SpringerBriefs in Economics



For further volumes:
http://www.springer.com/series/8876

Rajarshi Majumder

# Intergenerational Mobility

## A Study of Social Classes in India

Springer

Rajarshi Majumder
Department of Economics
University of Burdwan
Burdwan, West Bengal
India

ISSN 2191-5504 ISSN 2191-5512 (electronic)
ISBN 978-81-322-1129-7 ISBN 978-81-322-1130-3 (eBook)
DOI 10.1007/978-81-322-1130-3
Springer New Delhi Heidelberg New York Dordrecht London

Library of Congress Control Number: 2013933584



Printed on acid-free paper

Springer is part of Springer Science+Business Media (www.springer.com)

# Acknowledgments

I was sensitised to the issue of disparities across social classes in India by none other than Prof. SK Thorat, my teacher at JNU, later Chairman of University Grants Commission of India and presently Chairman, Indian Council of Social Science Research. During my long periods of research on this disparity as manifested in the labour market, I was perplexed by the fact that a majority of the lagging social classes seem to have remained stuck in traditional low paying occupations over generations and rarely imbibe human capital so necessary today for climbing up the socioeconomic ladder. The seeds of the current research were sown then, which I pursued with financial assistance from the University Grants Commission. I am thankful to UGC for the financial support. I also wish to thank Koushik Hati and Krishanu Sarkar, Project Fellows at the Department of Economics, University of Burdwan, for assisting in conducting the field surveys, computation and tabulation of data, and research assistance. Officials at the district offices of West Bengal SC and ST Development and Financial Corporation at Bardhaman and Bankura helped in designing the surveys and providing background information on various schemes of the government aimed at occupational transformation of the lagging social classes. My postgraduate students at the department carried on the field surveys with rare enthusiasm and their bubbling energy were a joy to watch and share. Academic exchanges with Dipa Mukherjee, Amaresh Dubey, Pinaki Chakraborti and Jhilam Ray have been most invigorating. Remaining deficiencies are of the author.

# Contents

# Abstract

Discrimination and exclusion in the process of capability formation and labour market transcends the boundary of the current generation and spills over to successive generations as well. Naturally, this results in low intergenerational mobility among the historically oppressed classes of society, especially in developing countries. Though a plethora of work has been done at the international level, the area has remained under-focussed in Indian economic research. This is quite unexpected since social exclusion and disparity have been quite substantial in India and none have had as long-lasting an effect as the division along caste lines. The present monograph addresses this research gap and explores the issue of intergenerational mobility in the Indian context across different social classes, analysing the spheres of both education and occupation. It is observed that though some improvement has been made by the current generation over the previous one, upward mobility has been limited to mainly educational levels and the advanced social classes. Parental education and occupation has a significantly greater impact on educational attainment and occupational choice for socially excluded groups compared to the advanced groups. In the labour market, much of the intergenerational mobility is lateral and not vertical. Regional pattern suggests that mobility rates in general are lower in most of the lagging states. This lack of upward mobility, especially among the socially excluded classes, is a matter of grave concern. The fact that educational mobility is not being transformed to occupational mobility also brings up the possibility of discrimination in the labour market. The results bear testimony to the fact that historical discrimination and social exclusion have had a long-run effect and it is very difficult to come out of this inertia. Focussed affirmative action and state support needs to be pursued to break this stagnancy.

**Keywords** Intergenerational mobility · Social exclusion · Discrimination · Educational standard · Occupational structure

# Abstract

[illegible]

# Introduction

## Background

Several social classes, especially in developing countries, are often excluded from the process of capability formation and income-earning opportunities due to various forms of discrimination. This exclusion and backwardness transcends the boundary of the current generation and spills over to successive generations as well. Consequently, Intergenerational Mobility in terms of both Education and Occupation is very low among backward classes. This leads to substantial social exclusion through which individuals or groups are wholly or partially excluded from the society in which they live (De Haan and Maxwell 1998). Such social exclusion focuses attention on central aspects of deprivation, is equally relevant to analysis and policies, and directs us to the fact that deprivation is a multi-generational—multidimensional phenomenon. It is also linked to social and political capital formation, particularly in terms of policies for alleviating social dimensions of poverty. The World Bank (2000) has accepted the overlapping generation impact of social exclusion by commenting:

> Discrimination on the basis of gender, ethnicity, race, religion, or social status can lead to social exclusion and lock people into long-term poverty traps.

This process of exclusion can be linked to deprivation or impoverishment in a multi-dimensional and interactional fashion, rather than in a linear way. On one hand, the 'poor' are likely to be excluded from wider participation in society because of their relative material disadvantage in terms of income. On the other, exclusion from the avenues of capability formation due to low income also renders them poorly endowed in terms of human capital and hence reduces the income of their next generation. Under such circumstances it becomes imperative to understand the absence of intergenerational educational and occupational mobility among socially backward classes vis-à-vis the advanced groups.

Of all the lines along which exclusion and disparity have been practiced in India none have had as long-lasting an effect as the division along caste lines. The Scheduled Castes and Tribes, along with the Other Backward Castes (OBCs) have been a pariah in the development process of India for quite a long time. Affirmative


DOI: 10.1007/978-81-322-1130-3_1, 

action in the form of reservation in Education and Employment were taken after independence to provide them space in the mainstream and trigger self-sustaining growth of these groups. However, it is often argued that successive generations of the lagging classes (SCs, STs, and OBCs) are stuck at the same social status—Educational and Occupational. Intergenerational mobility among these classes is very low, unlike the other advanced or advantaged classes. In recent years the issue has again come to centre-stage in view of the debate between pro- and anti-reservation lobbies. Before aligning with any of the groups, one must first take a stock of the real situation of these socially excluded groups in terms of mobility across generations. And if indeed the mobility is relatively low, the causes for such low mobility have to be ascertained before drawing up effective policies for their upliftment. This monograph aims to be a small step towards that broad social goal. It is also pioneering since no such comprehensive and broad-based study exists in the Indian context till date, importance of caste notwithstanding.

## Caste Discrimination in India: Brief Historical Perspective

It has already been mentioned that social classification in India has been predominantly along lines of caste—differentiating the upper castes (general or advanced class) from the rest (Scheduled Castes, Other Backward Castes, and the *adivasis* or indigenous tribes). Evolution of this stratification can be traced back to around fifteenth century BC when the advent of the *Aryans* pushed the original inhabitants of the land into geographically isolated enclaves. These groups came to be known as *tribals*, had completely different social, economic and religious customs, did not practice settled agriculture. Their seclusion strengthened during the later Muslim and British rule. While difference between the Aryans and the Tribals created the primary divide, over time the Aryan society also became segregated, mainly on the basis of occupation. By first century AD five major caste groups were identified. In order of social hierarchy they were—the *Brahmins* (priests and teachers), the *Khsatriyas* (rulers and soldiers), the *Vaishyas* (traders and merchants), the *Shudras* (artisans and labourers), and the *Dalits* or 'Untouchables' (associate with tasks that were considered too polluting or filthy, e.g. scavenging). The first three comprised the traditional upper castes. According to social custom, a person is born into a caste and carries it till his death. Therefore caste can be defined as a system of segregating the society into rigid compartments based on traditional occupation, the system being hereditary, closed, exclusionary, and ritualistic. Social norms were rigid and since knowledge, power, and assets rested with the upper castes, the rest, especially the *Dalits* faced discrimination and ostracization in all spheres of life till the twentieth century. Since the original system was based on occupation and asset ownership in the first place and was hereditary, the disparities between the upper castes, *Shudras* and *Dalits* increased over time. The British rule strengthened the caste system and associated discrimination. First, the British codified and recorded caste in the decennial population census, creating indelible barriers in the society. Second, they co-opted members from the upper castes into their ruling coalition and the administrative hierarchy mirrored the existing social stratification. Princes, Teachers, and Landlords were the most privileged communities, and helped the British administration to govern. Next came the merchants who were part of the commercial network that the British used for extraction of surplus from the colony. Wage labourers, farmers, and servants came next, followed by the indentured labourers and coolies, who came mostly from the *shudra*, *dalit* and tribal communities. The colonial social strata therefore juxtaposed with the existing caste system, preventing social fluidity of the nature observed in the United States or Europe where the traditional stratification was not reinforced by colonial segregation. All the while the tribals became more and more disjointed from the mainstream society, lacked exposure to modern education or economic activities, and became part of the lagging social class in India. It was only after independence that India tried to reverse the exploitation of the *dalits* and the tribals by giving express recognition to more than 1 thousand castes and more than 7 hundred tribes in the First Schedule of its constitution in 1950. These groups came to be known as Scheduled Castes and Scheduled Tribes and various positive discrimination through reservation and quota in elementary education and government jobs were provided to bring them up to a level playing field. In 1993, the *shudras* were also brought under the purview of reservation by designating them as Other Backward Castes [for a detailed discussion see Ambedkar (1979); Hutton (1946); Smelser and Lipset (2005)].

Such positive steps notwithstanding, discrimination still exists in India in the form of 'hidden apartheid'. Members of upper castes, knowingly or unknowingly as part of social custom, discriminate against and exploit the lagging castes. The state interventions are too little too late, and it is still very difficult to break caste boundaries in India. Since caste is considered hereditary, advantages and disadvantages transmit from one generation to the next, projecting the upper castes to a virtuous self propelling upward spiral while trapping the backward castes in vicious cycle of low education-occupation-income.

## Review of Current Research

### *Empirical Experience: International*

Internationally, in economics, there is an extensive literature on the transmission of economic success from generation to generation. That the family plays a crucial role in shaping income inequality has long been recognised by economists (Knight 1935; Parsons 1975; Becker and Tomes 1979, 1986; Loury 1981). Hertz et al. (2007) estimated trends in intergenerational persistence of educational attainment for a sample of 42 nations around the globe over fifty year period and obtained large regional differences, with Latin America displaying the highest intergenerational correlations, and the Nordic countries the lowest. Most of the recent studies, e.g. Cheng (1995) for China, Behrman et al. (2001) for Latin America, Bowles and Gintis (2002) for the US, Bourguignon et al. (2003) for Brazil, Checchi et al. (2008) for Italy, conclude that there is both a significant direct and indirect effect of parental education/occupation/income on young people's educational attainment level, occupational destinations and well being [see Mazumder (2001) for a brief review]. On the other hand, low parental influence has been reported by Peters (1992) for the US, Gang and Zimmermann (1999) for immigrant Germans, Black et al. (2003) for Norway, Louw et al. (2006) for South Africa, and Brown et al. (2009) for Great Britain.

## *Empirical Experience: Indian Context*

One of the earliest works in Indian context has been that of Driver (1962). Using data on the male heads of households in Nagpur district, he concluded that intergenerational mobility is frequent among rural and urban castes but is generally confined to occupations of similar rank. This association was attributed by the author to differences among castes in educational attainment. Surprisingly, caste being such an important issue in India in determining various socio-economic and political dimensions, there has been only few studies to compare intergenerational mobility of various castes in India in recent times. Kumar et al. (2002a, b) discussed the role of caste and community in class mobility and the impact of modernisation on such processes using National Election Study data of 1971 and 1996 from 80 and 108 parliamentary constituencies respectively, across India. Using the mobility matrix, they infer that the dominant picture is that of continuity rather than mobility, though the stagnation is attributable to financial and other resource-related factors and not caste alone.

More recently Jalan and Murgai (2007) look at inequalities in educational outcomes across groups of individuals and the perpetuation of these inequalities across generations using NFHS data for 1992–1993 and 1998–1999 and conclude that educational mobility in India is up to international standards and has further increased over time. Also, the differences in mobility are more along Rich–Poor divide rather than along caste lines. Deshpande and Palshikar (2008) use survey data from Pune city to look at intergenerational occupational mobility across different castes and observe substantial upward mobility in the aggregate. Using both mobility matrix and regression techniques, they also infer that while caste does matter for upward mobility, in general occupational mobility across generations is not shaped by caste factors.

The studies on social disparity and labour market however are either case studies, or even when the study is of macro dimension are limited to studying the unemployment rates only without exploring the type of employment—the crux of disparity. Also, no effort has been made to understand how the inequality is behaving over generations or whether educational status and occupational status is substantially improving across generations for the backward classes.

It is thus evident that though a plethora of work has been done at the international level, especially in the developed countries context, the area has remained under-focussed in Indian economic research. Whether close to half a century of affirmative action have been able to create greater mobility among the *Excluded Castes* (EC hereafter, comprising of SC, ST and OBCs taken together) and bring in higher social fluidity in the nation as a whole, remains an important area to be explored.

The present study will try to fill in this void in existing literature by bringing out not only the educational attainment level and occupational structure among various castes in India, but also the degree of educational and occupational mobility for them, disaggregated across gender wherever possible. The study is thus significant from the viewpoint of both assessing the current dispensation and understanding the temporal dynamics, not only from the economic point of view but also from the broader perspective of long run social justice and equity.

With identity politics taking centre-stage in the South Asian sub-continent, addressing issues of exclusion and stagnancy among specific socio-cultural groups is extremely important to pre-empt chances of unrest and instability in the world's largest multi-cultural democracy. The current political and sociological discourses are therefore expected to be modified according to the findings of the present study.

## Objectives

The broad goal of understanding intergenerational mobility in India induces us to frame the objective of the study as follows:

- Determination of disparities among social groups in India regarding Educational Attainment and Occupational distribution;
- Determination of Mobility across generations in terms of Educational Attainments and Occupational Status separately for the different social groups;
- Exploring whether the Mobility Rates are different for the two groups;
- Indicating some of the factors causing such disparities in Intergenerational mobility; and,
- Exploring whether state policies have succeeded in improving the occupational status of backward groups.

## Methodology and Database

How do we define the different social classes in India? Social Class in this study has been interchangeably used with *Caste*. In Indian socio-cultural milieu, the Scheduled Tribes (indigenous tribes), Scheduled Castes (the *Harijans*), and the

OBCs (*Dalits*) are generally compartmentalised as the *Lagging Classes* or the *Excluded Classes*, whereas the Upper Caste Hindus are the *Advanced Classes*. We follow the same notional nomenclature in this study.

Studies on Intergenerational transmission of educational and occupational characteristics have mostly followed two methodological approaches. The first type cross tabulates the individual characteristics with those of their parents and computes a Mobility Matrix, based on which proportion of people exhibiting Upward Mobility (children having higher educational/occupational position compared to their parents) are calculated. Starting with Driver (1962), this method has been used by Erikson and Goldthorpe (1992, 2002), Cheng (1995), Biblarz (1996), Kumar (2002), Behrman et al. (2001), Beller and Hout (2006), and Louw et al. (2006). This is basically a descriptive approach without analysing the impact of other variables on such transmission. When computed separately across social groups, it provides measures of upward mobility for each of them, which can then be compared. However, this method is unable to bring out the causal relation between parental educational and occupational status and that of the children objectively when several other possible explanatory factors are present. This gives rise to the second method which is more rigorous in nature and typically regress child's educational/occupational characteristics on those of the parents along with a set of other control variables. The coefficients of parental characteristics will give us a measure of intergenerational inertia in our dependent variable. A high coefficient will denote low mobility while a low coefficient will represent high mobility. Apart from OLS Regression, Logistic Regression and Correlation has also been used to objectively measure parental influence on children's achievement level using this method. Researchers using this methodology include Behrman and Wolfe (1984), Solon (1992), Peters (1992), Gang and Zimmermann (1999), Bowles and Gintis (2002), Bourguignon et al. (2003), Black et al. (2003), Checchi et al. (2008), and Brown et al. (2009). While the Mobility Matrix method has been used mostly for case studies when achievement levels are discrete categories in hierarchically ordered classes (e.g. occupational category), the Regression/Correlation method has been used when a large dataset has been available and achievement levels are measured in continuous scale (e.g. income or completed years of schooling). Though the regression/correlation approach has been in favour in recent times, it is sometimes criticised on the ground that the association between parental and children's achievements is non-linear over the achievements range of parents and hence cannot be truly captured by this method (Bjorklund and Jantti 2000). For these reasons, we have used both the approaches in the present paper—first calculating upward mobility across generations separately for different social groups from the mobility matrix and comparing them; then attempting an econometric exercise where individual educational/occupational attainments have been expressed as function of parental achievements; to bring out the dynamics of intergenerational mobility.

The study has used both Secondary and Primary Field Data. The database on employment and unemployment (Unit level records) obtained from the National Sample Survey Office (NSSO) is the main secondary data source. NSSO data for the years 1993–94 and 2004–05 pertaining to the 50th and 61st round surveys were used (NSSO 1997, 2006). These are large sample surveys conducted throughout India with a structured questionnaire. While the 1993 survey covered 115,409 households enumerating 564,740 persons, spread over 6,983 villages and 4,670 urban blocks, the 2004 survey was spread over 7,999 villages and 4,602 urban blocks covering 124,680 households and 602,833 persons.[1]

We processed, tabulated, and analysed these vast database using modern Computing and DBMS facilities. Once the various tables were ready they were analysed using econometric tools, and the trends, variations, interactions were explored using Statistical and Econometric techniques.

It was followed by Primary Survey in selected localities of three districts of South West Bengal—Purulia, Bankura and Bardhaman where substantial numbers of Scheduled Castes, Tribes and OBCs are present for a long time. Intergenerational mobility in terms of Education and Occupation for these groups was determined from the field survey. A control group of general caste were used to bring out the differences between the two groups, especially to understand the reasons for lack of intergenerational mobility among the backward classes. With this background, we now explore the situation in India from next chapter onwards.

## References


Ambedkar BR (1979) Castes in india: their mechanism, genesis and development. In: Babasaheb Ambedkar (ed) Writings and Speeches, vol I. Education Dept., Government of Maharashtra, Bombay

Becker GS, Tomes N (1979) An equilibrium theory of the distribution of income and intergenerational mobility. J Polit Econ 87(6):1153–1189

Becker GS, Tomes N (1986) Human capital and the rise and fall of families. J Labor Econ 4:S1–S39

Behrman JR, Gaviria A, Miguel S (2001) Intergenerational mobility in Latin America. Working Paper Number 352, Inter-american development bank, research department. www.iadb.org/res/publications/pubfiles/pubWP-452.pdf. Accessed on 26 Oct 2009

Behrman JR, Wolfe BL (1984) The socioeconomic impact of schooling in a developing country. The Rev Econ Stat 66–2:296–303

Beller E, Hout M (2006) Intergenerational social mobility: the United States in comparative perspective. The Future Child 16–2:19–36

Biblarz TJ, Bengtson VL, Bucur A (1996) Social mobility across three generations. J Marriage Fam 58–1:188–200

Bjorklund A, Jantti M (2000) Intergenerational mobility of socio-economic status in comparative perspective. Nord J Polit Econ 26–1:3–33

Black SE, Devereux PJ, Salvanes KG (2003) Why the apple doesn't fall far: understanding intergenerational transmission of human capital. IZA Discussion Paper No. 926, Nov

Bourguignon F, Ferreira FHG, Menéndez M (2003) Inequality of outcomes and inequality of opportunities in brazil. william davidson institute working paper number 630, Nov 2003. www.wdi.bus.umich.edu. Accessed on 30 Oct 2009

Bowles S, Gintis H (2002) The inheritance of inequality. The J Econ Perspect 16–3:3–30


[1] Details of the dataset are available from www.mospi.nic.in.

Brown S, McIntosh S, Taylor K (2009) Following in your parents' footsteps? empirical analysis of matched parent-offspring test scores. IZA Discussion Paper No. 3986, Jan 2009
Checchi D, Fiorio CV, Leonardi M (2008) Intergenerational persistence in educational attainment in Italy. IZA Discussion Paper No. 3622, July
Cheng Y, Dai J (1995) Intergenerational mobility in modern China. Eur Sociol Rev 11–1:17–35
De Haan A, Maxwell S (1998) Poverty and Social Exclusion in North and South. IDS Bulletin. 29–1:1–9
Deshpande R, Palshikar S (2008) Patterns of occupational mobility: how much does caste matter? Econ Polit Wkly 43–34:61–70
Driver ED (1962) Caste and occupational structure in central India. Soc Forces 41–1:26–31
Erikson R, Goldthorpe JH (1992) The constant flux: a study of class mobility in industrial societies. Clarendon Press, Oxford
Erikson R, Goldthorpe JH (2002) Intergenerational inequality: a sociological perspective. The J Econ Perspect 16–3:31–44
Gang IN, Zimmermann KF (1999) Is child like parent? educational attainment and ethnic origin. IZA Discussion Papers No 57:1999
Hertz T, Jayasundera T, Piraino P, Selcuk S, Smith N, Verashchagina A (2007) The inheritance of educational inequality: international comparisons and fifty-year trends. The B.E. J Econ Analysis Policy. pp 7–2 (Advances) Article 10. http://www.bepress.com/bejeap/vol7/iss2/art10. Accessed on 15 Dec 2008
Hutton JH (1946) Caste in India. Cambridge University Press, Cambridge
Jalan J, Murgai R (2007) Intergenerational mobility in education in India. (mimeo) World Bank, Delhi
Knight FH (1935) Professor Hayek and the theory of investment. Econ J 45–177:77–94
Kumar S, Heath A, Heath O (2002a) Determinants of social mobility in India. Econ Polit Wkly 37–29:2983–2987
Kumar S, Heath A, Heath O (2002b) Changing patterns of social mobility: some trends over time. Econ Polit Wkly 37–40:4091–4096
Loury GC (1981) Intergenerational transfers and the distribution of earnings. Econometrica 49–4:843–867
Louw M, van Der Berg S, Yu D (2006) Educational attainment and intergenerational social mobility in south africa. stellenbosch economic working papers number 09/06. www.ekon.sun.ac.za/wpapers/2006/wp092006/wp-09-2006.pdf. Accessed on 26 Oct 2009
Mazumder B (2001) Earnings mobility in the US: a new look at intergenerational inequality. center for labor research, University of California, Berkeley, Working Paper No. 34, Mar
Parsons DO (1975) Intergenerational wealth transfers and the educational decisions of male youth. Quart J Econ 89:603–617
Peters HE (1992) Patterns of intergenerational mobility in income and earnings. Rev Econ Stat 74–3:456–466
Smelser NJ, Lipset SM (2005) Social structure and mobility in economic development. Transaction Publishers, New Brunswick
Solon GR (1992) Intergenerational income mobility in the United States. Am Econ Rev 82–3:393–408
World Bank (2000) World Development Report 2000–2001: attacking poverty. World Bank

## Data Sources

NSSO (1997) Unit level records on sixth quinquennial survey on employment and unemployment in India 1993–1994 (Data on CD-ROM), NSS fiftieth round—July 1993–June 1994, National sample survey organisation, 1997. Government Of India, New Delhi

NSSO (2006) Unit level records on seventh quinquennial survey on employment and unemployment in India 2004–05 (Data on CD-ROM), NSS 61st Round—July 2004–June 2005, National Sample Survey Organisation, 2006. Government of India, New Delhi

National sample survey organisation, a unit of the ministry of statistics and program implementation, Government of India, has since been renamed as National sample survey office from April, 2010. Data used in this research is available on payment basis from NSSO. For details visit www.mospi.nic.in

# Education and Occupation in India

## Educational Status and Social Class

Educational attainment levels in India are substantially lower by international standards. Even in 2004, more than 30 % of the people are illiterate, and only about 20 % have completed secondary schooling.[1] Within such low standards, the situations of the *Excluded Castes* are still worse. 45 % of OBCs, 60 % of STs, and 55 % of SCs are illiterate, compared to only 27 % for the *Advanced Castes* (Table 1). Secondary schools have been completed by only about 8–11 % of the excluded class workers. If we consider different Gender classes, it is observed that women are placed much below the men. While 16 % of males are illiterate, more than 38 % of females are illiterate. At the other end of the scale, only about 20 % of females have passed secondary schools and above compared to 35 % of males. There are however disparities among different generations and age groups regarding educational levels. Children and young people are having better educational levels than their parents and older age group persons (Fig. 1). Also, standards have improved over the 1993–2004 period. Alarmingly, gender discrimination is pretty strong and illiteracy among Daughters is more than double compared to that among Sons. The upward mobility witnessed is more prominent among the advanced castes and marginal among the excluded castes, especially for the women.

## Occupational Hierarchy

One of the major factors affecting income distribution is the hierarchical structure of different occupations and the occupational distribution of the workers. Occupational segregation leads to perpetuation and also accentuation of income

[1] From the NSSO data, individuals can be grouped into any of the following Educational categories—Illiterate, Literate but below Primary level education, Primary School (Class 5) Passed, Middle School (Class 8) Passed, Secondary School (Class 10) Passed, Higher Secondary (Class 12) Passed, Graduate and above.

R. Majumder, *Intergenerational Mobility*, SpringerBriefs in Economics,
DOI: 10.1007/978-81-322-1130-3_2, 

**Table 1** **a, b** Educational attributes of different generation groups in India—1993–2004 (%), **c** Educational attributes of different age groups in India: 1993–2004 (%)

| Generation group | Educational group | 1993 | | | | 2004 | | | |
|---|---|---|---|---|---|---|---|---|---|
| | | ST | SC | OBC | GEN | ST | SC | OBC | GEN |
| (a) | | | | | | | | | |
| All | Illiterate | 50.1 | 41.0 | na | 20.9 | 60.5 | 55.2 | 44.8 | 26.8 |
| | Literate below Pr | 8.2 | 8.4 | na | 6.6 | 11.2 | 10.2 | 10.5 | 9.5 |
| | Primary passed | 8.6 | 8.9 | na | 8.4 | 10.1 | 11.3 | 12.7 | 12.6 |
| | Middle passed | 15.9 | 19.6 | na | 22.1 | 9.2 | 11.3 | 14.1 | 15.3 |
| | Secondary passed | 8.0 | 11.2 | na | 17.6 | 3.7 | 5.3 | 7.7 | 12.5 |
| | Hr Sec passed | 6.4 | 7.6 | na | 12.2 | 2.6 | 3.3 | 4.6 | 8.3 |
| | Grad and above | 2.9 | 3.4 | na | 12.2 | 2.6 | 3.4 | 5.6 | 14.9 |
| Fathers | Illiterate | 71.3 | 66.3 | na | 40.2 | 60.7 | 56.0 | 43.6 | 25.1 |
| | Literate below Pr | 13.7 | 15.6 | na | 18.9 | 15.5 | 14.1 | 16.1 | 13.4 |
| | Primary passed | 8.2 | 8.7 | na | 14.1 | 11.8 | 11.3 | 14.6 | 15.2 |
| | Middle passed | 3.3 | 5.3 | na | 10.6 | 6.0 | 8.1 | 11.2 | 14.2 |
| | Secondary passed | 2.0 | 2.6 | na | 8.7 | 2.9 | 5.5 | 7.3 | 14.4 |
| | Hr Sec passed | 0.8 | 0.9 | na | 3.0 | 1.0 | 2.2 | 3.1 | 6.2 |
| | Grad and above | 0.7 | 0.6 | na | 4.5 | 2.2 | 2.8 | 4.1 | 11.5 |
| Mothers | Illiterate | 90.2 | 89.0 | na | 68.7 | 86.8 | 83.8 | 74.4 | 52.2 |
| | Literate below Pr | 4.3 | 5.6 | na | 10.9 | 4.6 | 6.3 | 8.3 | 12.1 |
| | Primary passed | 2.8 | 3.3 | na | 9.4 | 4.3 | 5.0 | 8.5 | 13.2 |
| | Middle passed | 1.6 | 1.3 | na | 5.9 | 2.6 | 3.0 | 5.1 | 10.0 |
| | Secondary passed | 0.9 | 0.6 | na | 3.3 | 0.7 | 1.3 | 2.3 | 6.2 |
| | Hr Sec passed | 0.2 | 0.1 | na | 0.8 | 0.5 | 0.4 | 0.8 | 2.2 |
| | Grad and above | 0.1 | 0.1 | na | 1.0 | 0.5 | 0.2 | 0.6 | 4.0 |
| (b) | | | | | | | | | |
| All | Illiterate | 50.1 | 41.0 | na | 20.9 | 60.5 | 55.2 | 44.8 | 26.8 |
| | Literate below Pr | 8.2 | 8.4 | na | 6.6 | 11.2 | 10.2 | 10.5 | 9.5 |
| | Primary passed | 8.6 | 8.9 | na | 8.4 | 10.1 | 11.3 | 12.7 | 12.6 |
| | Middle passed | 15.9 | 19.6 | na | 22.1 | 9.2 | 11.3 | 14.1 | 15.3 |
| | Secondary passed | 8.0 | 11.2 | na | 17.6 | 3.7 | 5.3 | 7.7 | 12.5 |
| | Hr Sec passed | 6.4 | 7.6 | na | 12.2 | 2.6 | 3.3 | 4.6 | 8.3 |
| | Grad and above | 2.9 | 3.4 | na | 12.2 | 2.6 | 3.4 | 5.6 | 14.9 |
| Sons | Illiterate | 33.7 | 43.5 | na | 17.9 | 26.3 | 20.1 | 14.9 | 7.8 |
| | Literate below Pr | 12.3 | 12.7 | na | 9.6 | 13.8 | 10.5 | 8.8 | 6.5 |
| | Primary passed | 14.5 | 13.9 | na | 12.8 | 17.6 | 16.2 | 14.5 | 10.8 |
| | Middle passed | 17.2 | 14.0 | na | 19.6 | 20.3 | 23.4 | 24.5 | 19.2 |
| | Secondary passed | 10.6 | 7.7 | na | 16.5 | 9.6 | 11.7 | 14.3 | 17.4 |
| | Hr Sec passed | 8.2 | 6.0 | na | 12.3 | 6.7 | 9.5 | 10.7 | 15.6 |
| | Grad and above | 3.6 | 2.2 | na | 11.3 | 5.8 | 8.7 | 12.3 | 22.8 |
| Daughters | Illiterate | 67.3 | 73.0 | na | 42.0 | 49.9 | 45.7 | 37.5 | 15.8 |
| | Literate below Pr | 8.8 | 6.9 | na | 9.4 | 11.2 | 9.4 | 9.1 | 7.0 |
| | Primary passed | 8.3 | 7.8 | na | 10.8 | 10.6 | 11.8 | 12.5 | 11.8 |
| | Middle passed | 7.9 | 6.0 | na | 12.9 | 14.3 | 14.2 | 17.2 | 18.5 |
| | Secondary passed | 4.4 | 2.9 | na | 10.0 | 5.4 | 7.2 | 9.5 | 13.8 |
| | Hr Sec passed | 2.3 | 2.1 | na | 6.9 | 4.2 | 5.6 | 6.6 | 12.2 |
| | Grad and above | 1.0 | 1.3 | na | 7.9 | 4.4 | 6.0 | 7.6 | 20.9 |

(continued)

**Table 1** (continued)

| Age Cohort | Educational group | 1993 | | | | 2004 | | | |
|---|---|---|---|---|---|---|---|---|---|
| | | ST | SC | OBC | GEN | ST | SC | OBC | GEN |
| (c) | | | | | | | | | |
| All | Illiterate | 50.1 | 41.0 | na | 20.9 | 60.5 | 55.2 | 44.8 | 26.8 |
| | Literate below Pr | 8.2 | 8.4 | na | 6.6 | 11.2 | 10.2 | 10.5 | 9.5 |
| | Primary passed | 8.6 | 8.9 | na | 8.4 | 10.1 | 11.3 | 12.7 | 12.6 |
| | Middle passed | 15.9 | 19.6 | na | 22.1 | 9.2 | 11.3 | 14.1 | 15.3 |
| | Secondary passed | 8.0 | 11.2 | na | 17.6 | 3.7 | 5.3 | 7.7 | 12.5 |
| | Hr Sec passed | 6.4 | 7.6 | na | 12.2 | 2.6 | 3.3 | 4.6 | 8.3 |
| | Grad and above | 2.9 | 3.4 | na | 12.2 | 2.6 | 3.4 | 5.6 | 14.9 |
| 20–40 | Illiterate | 59.4 | 50.6 | na | 29.6 | 53.0 | 45.6 | 35.8 | 19.9 |
| | Literate below Pr | 9.7 | 10.7 | na | 9.7 | 12.1 | 10.9 | 10.2 | 8.4 |
| | Primary passed | 10.4 | 11.5 | na | 12.4 | 11.6 | 13.2 | 13.8 | 12.8 |
| | Middle passed | 9.8 | 12.7 | na | 16.7 | 11.9 | 14.7 | 17.6 | 17.4 |
| | Secondary passed | 4.9 | 7.4 | na | 13.2 | 4.7 | 6.8 | 9.4 | 13.9 |
| | Hr Sec passed | 4.0 | 5.0 | na | 9.3 | 3.5 | 4.6 | 6.1 | 10.7 |
| | Grad and above | 1.8 | 2.2 | na | 9.2 | 3.2 | 4.4 | 7.1 | 17.0 |
| 40+ | Illiterate | 73.9 | 76.7 | na | 46.2 | 70.8 | 67.1 | 54.6 | 32.9 |
| | Literate below Pr | 12.6 | 8.0 | na | 10.0 | 10.4 | 10.0 | 11.2 | 10.5 |
| | Primary passed | 6.9 | 5.6 | na | 11.8 | 8.0 | 9.2 | 11.8 | 12.5 |
| | Middle passed | 2.5 | 6.5 | na | 11.0 | 5.1 | 6.8 | 10.1 | 13.7 |
| | Secondary passed | 3.2 | 1.8 | na | 9.7 | 2.3 | 3.4 | 5.8 | 11.0 |
| | Hr Sec passed | 0.0 | 0.6 | na | 4.0 | 1.3 | 1.5 | 2.6 | 5.7 |
| | Grad and above | 0.9 | 0.9 | na | 7.2 | 1.9 | 2.1 | 3.7 | 13.8 |

*Source* Author's calculations based on data sources mentioned in the text

inequality over generations. Therefore, examining the occupational distribution of workers becomes an important issue.

We have used the Indian NCO-1968 classification in our study and workers have been divided into 10 occupational classes. Arranged in descending order of hierarchy, average remuneration, and prestige, these are—Technical and Scientific Personnel, Professionals, Administrative workers, Clerical workers, Sales workers, Service workers, Farmers, Production related workers, Transport workers, and Labourers not elsewhere classified. Occupational structure and mobility is discussed in terms of this structure. We have at the second level clubbed similar occupations to form 3 broad groups—Grade-I (White Collar jobs—Technical and Scientific Personnel, Professionals, and Administrative workers); Grade-II (Pink Collar Jobs—Clerical, Sales, and Service workers); and Grade-III (Blue Collar jobs—Farmers, Production related workers, Transport workers, and Labourers not elsewhere classified). This hierarchical structure has also been used in our study.

It is observed that the workers of the *Excluded Castes* are much more concentrated in Grade-III jobs compared to the *Advanced Castes*, while the proportion of the latter in Grade-I jobs is unduly large (Tables 2 and 3). In 2004, more than 90 % of the backward class workers were engaged in Grade-III occupations and only about 4–7 % in Grade-1 occupations. Contrary to this, just about 50 % of the

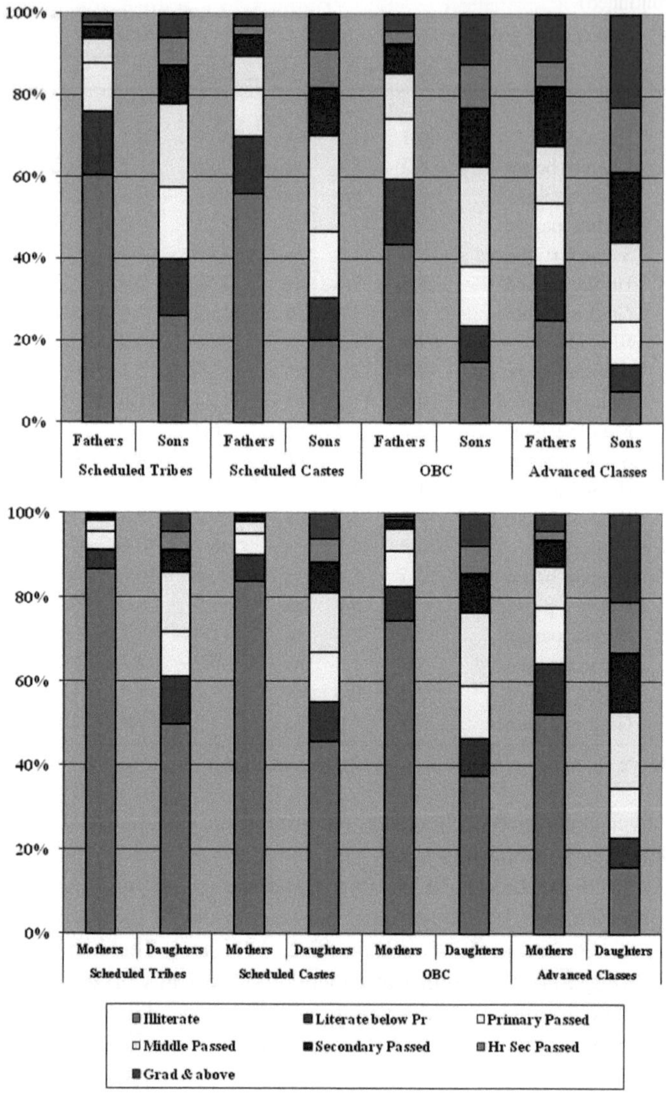


**Fig. 1** Educational qualifications of 20+ population in India across generations—2004. *Source* Author's calculations based on data sources mentioned in the text

advanced class workers were in Grade-III jobs and more than 15 % were in Grade-I jobs. What is more disheartening is to note that over the 1993–2004 period, the occupational structure of excluded social groups have shifted more towards Grade-III workers while that of the socially advanced groups have improved. This talks of increasing disparity in the labour market and reinforcement of exclusion along lines of caste in India in recent times.

**Table 2 a, b, c** Occupational attributes (1-digit NOC) of different groups in India: 1993–2004 (%)

| Generation group | Occupational group | 1993 | | | | 2004 | | | |
|---|---|---|---|---|---|---|---|---|---|
| | | ST | SC | OBC | GEN | ST | SC | OBC | GEN |
| (a) | | | | | | | | | |
| All | Technical | 4.3 | 5.4 | na | 4.8 | 1.1 | 1.5 | 1.6 | 2.6 |
| | Professionals | 1.7 | 1.8 | na | 4.8 | 1.6 | 1.7 | 2.3 | 6.1 |
| | Administrative | 2.1 | 1.0 | na | 3.8 | 1.2 | 1.6 | 3.0 | 6.8 |
| | Clerical | 1.4 | 2.9 | na | 5.4 | 1.3 | 2.1 | 2.4 | 5.0 |
| | Sales | 3.5 | 6.0 | na | 13.1 | 2.8 | 4.8 | 7.9 | 12.8 |
| | Service | 1.4 | 5.0 | na | 3.5 | 1.8 | 5.7 | 4.4 | 3.7 |
| | Farmers | 65.2 | 48.6 | na | 38.8 | 76.0 | 57.3 | 57.2 | 44.1 |
| | Production etc. | 11.3 | 21.0 | na | 20.0 | 7.9 | 18.0 | 16.8 | 14.0 |
| | Transport | 0.9 | 2.7 | na | 3.0 | 1.2 | 3.1 | 2.6 | 3.3 |
| | Labourers nec | 8.1 | 5.7 | na | 2.7 | 5.0 | 4.1 | 2.0 | 1.8 |
| Fathers | Technical | 1.8 | 2.4 | na | 2.4 | 0.7 | 1.1 | 0.9 | 2.3 |
| | Professionals | 0.9 | 1.2 | na | 3.4 | 1.4 | 1.6 | 1.6 | 5.1 |
| | Administrative | 0.5 | 1.1 | na | 3.4 | 0.9 | 2.3 | 3.7 | 7.6 |
| | Clerical | 1.9 | 2.5 | na | 3.8 | 1.9 | 3.7 | 2.7 | 4.7 |
| | Sales | 2.1 | 4.6 | na | 9.4 | 1.9 | 4.7 | 8.4 | 13.0 |
| | Service | 1.0 | 4.0 | na | 2.8 | 0.9 | 5.2 | 3.6 | 2.6 |
| | Farmers | 83.0 | 67.7 | na | 62.4 | 83.1 | 58.7 | 64.0 | 53.1 |
| | Production etc. | 5.4 | 12.4 | na | 9.8 | 6.5 | 15.7 | 12.4 | 8.7 |
| | Transport | 0.6 | 1.4 | na | 1.4 | 0.7 | 3.3 | 1.7 | 1.9 |
| | Labourers nec | 2.7 | 2.7 | na | 1.1 | 1.9 | 3.6 | 0.9 | 0.8 |
| Mothers | Technical | 2.3 | 4.0 | na | 4.1 | 1.4 | 1.6 | 1.8 | 1.5 |
| | Professionals | 0.3 | 0.2 | na | 2.8 | 0.7 | 0.4 | 0.7 | 3.8 |
| | Administrative | 0.8 | 1.1 | na | 1.4 | 0.5 | 1.6 | 1.5 | 2.9 |
| | Clerical | 0.3 | 0.6 | na | 1.1 | 0.3 | 1.0 | 0.7 | 2.0 |
| | Sales | 3.7 | 3.1 | na | 4.3 | 1.8 | 2.8 | 4.8 | 5.2 |
| | Service | 1.4 | 5.9 | na | 3.4 | 1.3 | 10.5 | 4.4 | 3.5 |
| | Farmers | 87.5 | 76.1 | na | 75.1 | 90.0 | 73.3 | 77.8 | 71.3 |
| | Production etc. | 3.1 | 7.8 | na | 7.1 | 3.0 | 7.6 | 7.9 | 8.7 |
| | Transport | 0.1 | 0.0 | na | 0.0 | 0.0 | 0.0 | 0.0 | 0.1 |
| | Labourers nec | 0.6 | 1.1 | na | 0.7 | 1.0 | 1.2 | 0.5 | 1.1 |
| (b) | | | | | | | | | |
| All | Technical | 4.3 | 5.4 | na | 4.8 | 1.1 | 1.5 | 1.6 | 2.6 |
| | Professionals | 1.7 | 1.8 | na | 4.8 | 1.6 | 1.7 | 2.3 | 6.1 |
| | Administrative | 2.1 | 1.0 | na | 3.8 | 1.2 | 1.6 | 3.0 | 6.8 |
| | Clerical | 1.4 | 2.9 | na | 5.4 | 1.3 | 2.1 | 2.4 | 5.0 |
| | Sales | 3.5 | 6.0 | na | 13.1 | 2.8 | 4.8 | 7.9 | 12.8 |
| | Service | 1.4 | 5.0 | na | 3.5 | 1.8 | 5.7 | 4.4 | 3.7 |
| | Farmers | 65.2 | 48.6 | na | 38.8 | 76.0 | 57.3 | 57.2 | 44.1 |
| | Production etc. | 11.3 | 21.0 | na | 20.0 | 7.9 | 18.0 | 16.8 | 14.0 |
| | Transport | 0.9 | 2.7 | na | 3.0 | 1.2 | 3.1 | 2.6 | 3.3 |
| | Labourers nec | 8.1 | 5.7 | na | 2.7 | 5.0 | 4.1 | 2.0 | 1.8 |

(continued)

**Table 2** (continued)

| Generation group/Age Cohort | Occupational group | 1993 | | | | 2004 | | | |
|---|---|---|---|---|---|---|---|---|---|
| | | ST | SC | OBC | GEN | ST | SC | OBC | GEN |
| Sons | Technical | 3.0 | 2.2 | na | 3.0 | 1.1 | 1.8 | 1.8 | 2.2 |
| | Professionals | 1.2 | 0.9 | na | 2.5 | 1.5 | 2.3 | 2.4 | 4.1 |
| | Administrative | 0.8 | 0.4 | na | 2.8 | 1.4 | 1.8 | 3.2 | 6.4 |
| | Clerical | 1.7 | 0.8 | na | 2.9 | 1.1 | 1.7 | 1.9 | 3.2 |
| | Sales | 5.2 | 2.1 | na | 11.5 | 3.1 | 7.0 | 11.1 | 17.3 |
| | Service | 2.4 | 0.8 | na | 2.3 | 1.8 | 4.0 | 3.5 | 1.9 |
| | Farmers | 64.3 | 77.3 | na | 56.3 | 70.5 | 49.7 | 52.3 | 44.2 |
| | Production etc. | 14.8 | 8.5 | na | 14.0 | 10.4 | 22.0 | 18.0 | 14.4 |
| | Transport | 2.0 | 0.9 | na | 2.5 | 1.9 | 4.3 | 3.7 | 4.0 |
| | Labourers nec | 4.6 | 6.2 | na | 2.2 | 7.2 | 5.4 | 2.2 | 2.3 |
| Daughters | Technical | 5.7 | 3.3 | na | 4.5 | 1.7 | 1.5 | 2.5 | 2.1 |
| | Professionals | 1.4 | 0.9 | na | 4.2 | 1.6 | 2.9 | 4.3 | 13.0 |
| | Administrative | 0.2 | 1.8 | na | 1.2 | 0.2 | 1.5 | 1.4 | 3.6 |
| | Clerical | 0.2 | 0.2 | na | 1.9 | 0.5 | 0.5 | 1.4 | 3.2 |
| | Sales | 0.6 | 1.5 | na | 1.5 | 0.6 | 2.1 | 2.3 | 2.5 |
| | Service | 3.4 | 0.9 | na | 1.9 | 1.0 | 4.0 | 2.0 | 1.9 |
| | Farmers | 78.8 | 85.6 | na | 74.0 | 85.8 | 74.0 | 74.3 | 62.0 |
| | Production etc. | 7.9 | 3.7 | na | 9.8 | 4.8 | 12.1 | 11.3 | 10.9 |
| | Transport | 0.1 | 0.0 | na | 0.0 | 0.0 | 0.2 | 0.1 | 0.3 |
| | Labourers nec | 1.7 | 2.2 | na | 1.0 | 3.9 | 1.0 | 0.5 | 0.5 |
| (c) | | | | | | | | | |
| All | Technical | 4.3 | 5.4 | na | 4.8 | 1.1 | 1.5 | 1.6 | 2.6 |
| | Professionals | 1.7 | 1.8 | na | 4.8 | 1.6 | 1.7 | 2.3 | 6.1 |
| | Administrative | 2.1 | 1.0 | na | 3.8 | 1.2 | 1.6 | 3.0 | 6.8 |
| | Clerical | 1.4 | 2.9 | na | 5.4 | 1.3 | 2.1 | 2.4 | 5.0 |
| | Sales | 3.5 | 6.0 | na | 13.1 | 2.8 | 4.8 | 7.9 | 12.8 |
| | Service | 1.4 | 5.0 | na | 3.5 | 1.8 | 5.7 | 4.4 | 3.7 |
| | Farmers | 65.2 | 48.6 | na | 38.8 | 76.0 | 57.3 | 57.2 | 44.1 |
| | Production etc. | 11.3 | 21.0 | na | 20.0 | 7.9 | 18.0 | 16.8 | 14.0 |
| | Transport | 0.9 | 2.7 | na | 3.0 | 1.2 | 3.1 | 2.6 | 3.3 |
| | Labourers nec | 8.1 | 5.7 | na | 2.7 | 5.0 | 4.1 | 2.0 | 1.8 |
| 20–40 years | Technical | 2.7 | 3.4 | na | 3.4 | 1.1 | 1.5 | 1.8 | 2.5 |
| | Professionals | 1.0 | 1.2 | na | 3.3 | 1.8 | 2.0 | 2.6 | 6.0 |
| | Administrative | 1.3 | 0.7 | na | 2.7 | 1.2 | 1.5 | 3.0 | 6.5 |
| | Clerical | 0.8 | 2.0 | na | 3.8 | 1.1 | 1.8 | 2.0 | 4.5 |
| | Sales | 2.1 | 4.0 | na | 9.5 | 2.9 | 5.2 | 8.4 | 13.8 |
| | Service | 0.9 | 3.3 | na | 2.5 | 2.0 | 5.6 | 4.2 | 3.8 |
| | Farmers | 78.9 | 65.3 | na | 55.6 | 73.9 | 54.0 | 53.4 | 40.2 |
| | Production etc. | 6.8 | 14.3 | na | 14.8 | 8.6 | 20.1 | 19.1 | 16.7 |
| | Transport | 0.6 | 1.9 | na | 2.3 | 1.3 | 3.6 | 3.1 | 3.9 |
| | Labourers nec | 5.0 | 3.9 | na | 2.0 | 6.0 | 4.6 | 2.4 | 2.2 |

(continued)

**Table 2** (continued)

| Age Cohort | Occupational group | 1993 | | | | 2004 | | | |
|---|---|---|---|---|---|---|---|---|---|
| | | ST | SC | OBC | GEN | ST | SC | OBC | GEN |
| 40+ years | Technical | 1.8 | 4.9 | na | 3.4 | 1.1 | 1.4 | 1.3 | 2.9 |
| | Professionals | 1.6 | 0.9 | na | 4.1 | 1.5 | 1.5 | 1.9 | 6.6 |
| | Administrative | 0.9 | 0.3 | na | 2.3 | 1.2 | 1.7 | 3.0 | 7.6 |
| | Clerical | 1.3 | 0.9 | na | 3.6 | 2.0 | 3.1 | 3.4 | 6.5 |
| | Sales | 3.1 | 4.0 | na | 5.7 | 2.7 | 4.2 | 7.1 | 11.3 |
| | Service | 0.2 | 2.3 | na | 1.8 | 1.5 | 6.2 | 4.6 | 4.0 |
| | Farmers | 70.6 | 47.2 | na | 43.4 | 79.2 | 61.2 | 62.0 | 46.8 |
| | Production etc. | 6.8 | 7.5 | na | 6.0 | 6.7 | 15.0 | 13.4 | 10.3 |
| | Transport | 12.2 | 30.8 | na | 29.1 | 0.9 | 2.3 | 1.9 | 2.6 |
| | Labourers nec | 1.4 | 1.1 | na | 0.6 | 3.2 | 3.5 | 1.3 | 1.3 |

*Source* Author's calculations based on data sources mentioned in the text

**Table 3** Occupational attributes (occupational grade) of different groups in India—1993–2004

| Group | Occupational group | 1993 | | | | 2004 | | | |
|---|---|---|---|---|---|---|---|---|---|
| | | ST | SC | OBC | GEN | ST | SC | OBC | GEN |
| All | White | 9.1 | 9.6 | na | 15.5 | 4.0 | 4.8 | 6.9 | 15.5 |
| | Pink | 7.0 | 16.3 | na | 25.2 | 6.0 | 12.7 | 14.6 | 21.5 |
| | Blue | 83.9 | 74.1 | na | 59.3 | 90.0 | 82.5 | 78.5 | 63.1 |
| Fathers | White | 3.2 | 4.7 | na | 9.3 | 3.0 | 5.0 | 6.2 | 15.1 |
| | Pink | 5.0 | 11.1 | na | 16.1 | 4.7 | 13.6 | 14.7 | 20.3 |
| | Blue | 91.8 | 84.2 | na | 74.7 | 92.3 | 81.4 | 79.1 | 64.6 |
| Mothers | White | 3.4 | 5.4 | na | 8.3 | 2.6 | 3.6 | 4.0 | 8.2 |
| | Pink | 5.4 | 9.6 | na | 8.8 | 3.4 | 14.3 | 9.8 | 10.6 |
| | Blue | 91.3 | 85.0 | na | 82.9 | 94.0 | 82.1 | 86.2 | 81.2 |
| Sons | White | 5.1 | 3.5 | na | 8.2 | 4.0 | 5.9 | 7.4 | 12.6 |
| | Pink | 9.2 | 3.7 | na | 16.8 | 6.1 | 12.7 | 16.4 | 22.4 |
| | Blue | 85.7 | 92.9 | na | 75.0 | 89.9 | 81.4 | 76.2 | 65.0 |
| Daughters | White | 7.4 | 6.0 | na | 9.9 | 3.5 | 6.0 | 8.2 | 18.7 |
| | Pink | 4.2 | 2.6 | na | 5.3 | 2.1 | 6.7 | 5.6 | 7.6 |
| | Blue | 88.5 | 91.4 | na | 84.8 | 94.5 | 87.3 | 86.2 | 73.7 |
| 20–40 years | White | 4.9 | 5.3 | na | 9.5 | 4.1 | 5.0 | 7.3 | 14.9 |
| | Pink | 3.8 | 9.3 | na | 15.8 | 6.1 | 12.6 | 14.6 | 22.1 |
| | Blue | 91.3 | 85.4 | na | 74.7 | 89.8 | 82.4 | 78.1 | 63.0 |
| 40+ years | White | 4.9 | 8.8 | na | 13.7 | 3.8 | 4.5 | 6.3 | 17.1 |
| | Pink | 5.2 | 10.5 | na | 15.5 | 6.2 | 13.4 | 15.1 | 21.9 |
| | Blue | 89.8 | 80.7 | na | 70.8 | 90.0 | 82.0 | 78.6 | 61.0 |

*Source* Author's calculations based on data sources mentioned in the text

Some improvements in occupational structure are observed across generations whereby proportion of workers in hierarchically superior occupations is higher for the current generation of sons and daughters relative to their parents (Fig. 2). However, the rate of improvement is much more pronounced for the advanced

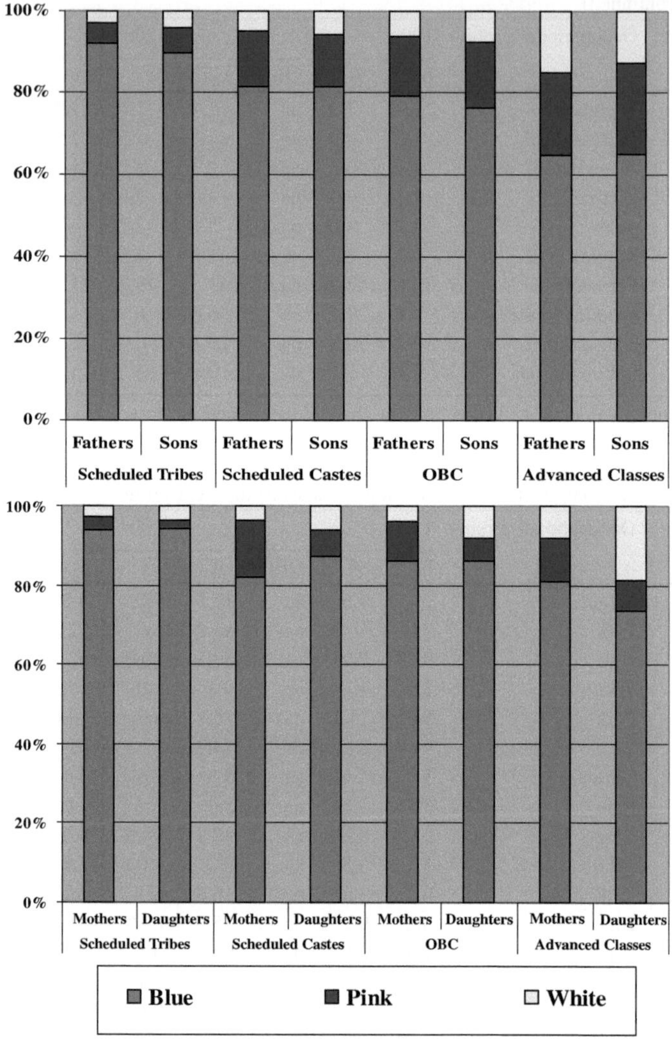


**Fig. 2** Broad occupational groups of 20+ workers in India across generations—2004. *Source* Author's calculations based on data sources mentioned in the text

castes. Moreover, share of workers in the Grade-III jobs have increased for the Parents and the Daughters belonging to Scheduled Tribes.

If we look at age groups instead of biological generations, similar picture emerges. Moving from population aged 40+ years to those between 20–40 years of age, there is a marginal upward movement among the OBCs, while for the SCs there is a tendency towards concentration in mid-level occupations. For the STs, there is a clear downward movement with proportion of Blue Collar workers increasing.

## Disparities: Statistical Examination

Results so far indicate that average educational and occupational levels of specific social classes are lower than others. However, to conclusively infer that there exist significant social disparity in terms of education and occupation, we must subject the data to rigorous statistical tests. We use the 2004 data for this exercise.

### *Educational Disparity*

Educational level was transformed to a new variable that indicates completed years of schooling and the averages were computed for each social group, separately for Parents and Children as also for the two age-cohorts. Since this is now a scale variable, average values can be compared using standard tests for comparing means (e.g. *t* test). Whether social group can explain differences in educational level can also be examined by analysing between and within group differences (e.g. ANOVA).

Paired *t* test were carried out with the General/Advanced Class as the reference group and differences in completed years of education between this group and the other social groups were tested for significance. It is observed that average educational level of the present generation (*children* group) is higher than that of the earlier one (*parents* group), which is quite expected (Table 4). Similarly, the

**Table 4** Educational disparity—paired *t* test results

| Group | Social groups | N (in millions) | Mean (Years) | SD | t-value | *p* value |
|---|---|---|---|---|---|---|
| Parents | General/advanced class[a] | 44,556 | 6.9 | 5.025 | | |
| | Scheduled tribe | 17,032 | 4.8 | 4.721 | 49.6** | 0.01 |
| | Scheduled caste | 21,058 | 3.8 | 4.432 | 80.5** | 0.01 |
| | Other backward classes | 48,687 | 4.9 | 4.707 | 61.5** | 0.01 |
| Children | General/advanced class[a] | 33,535 | 8.9 | 4.433 | | |
| | Scheduled tribe | 10,677 | 6.8 | 4.493 | 44.9** | 0.01 |
| | Scheduled caste | 12,499 | 6.3 | 4.697 | 53.7** | 0.01 |
| | Other backward classes | 34,362 | 7.2 | 4.672 | 47.3** | 0.01 |
| 20–40 age | General/advanced class[a] | 49,120 | 8.4 | 4.639 | | |
| | Scheduled tribe | 18,484 | 6.1 | 4.639 | 55.8** | 0.01 |
| | Scheduled caste | 22,027 | 5.5 | 4.702 | 74.9** | 0.01 |
| | Other backward classes | 53,663 | 6.7 | 4.734 | 57.8** | 0.01 |
| 40–60 age | General/advanced class[a] | 21,364 | 7.2 | 5.047 | | |
| | Scheduled tribe | 7,622 | 4.6 | 4.721 | 41.2** | 0.01 |
| | Scheduled caste | 8,957 | 3.6 | 4.407 | 63.2** | 0.01 |
| | Other backward classes | 22,193 | 4.9 | 4.752 | 48.7** | 0.01 |

*Note* a—Reference Group; Results for other social groups are paired against the control group; Dependent Variable—Average Years of Completed Education; Figures in Parenthesis are *p* values; ** indicates significance at 1 % level

younger cohort has better educational standard compared to the older one. However, our main interest is whether the gap between the advanced social class and the other three classes are statistically significant or not. It is observed that in all cases the reference group is significantly better than the three other social classes, as evident from statistically significant t-values. The gap is widest with the SCs and least with the OBCs. It is also evident that the gap has declined over generation/age cohort for the SCs and the OBCs, but has remained almost unchanged for the STs. This is clear proof of the relative stagnancy of the tribals in terms of education.

Tests involving ANOVA suggest that social group is an important factor in explaining differences in years of education as *between group* variations are significantly larger than corresponding *within group* variations (Table 5). Standard error from Games-Howell post-Hoc test confirms our inference that differences in educational levels among social groups are statistically significant (Table 6).

It is thus evident that the differences in average educational levels across social groups are systematic and statistically significant.

**Table 5** Educational disparity—ANOVA results

| Group | Sources of variance | Sum of square | Mean square | F-value | *p* value |
|---|---|---|---|---|---|
| Parents | Between groups | 173,023 | 57,674 | 2,527** | 0.01 |
| | Within groups | 2,997,015 | 23 | | |
| | Total | 3,170,038 | | | |
| Children | Between groups | 91,234 | 30,411 | 1,457** | 0.01 |
| | Within groups | 1,900,392 | 21 | | |
| | Total | 1,991,626 | | | |
| 20–40 age | Between groups | 159,395 | 53,132 | 2,421** | 0.01 |
| | Within groups | 3,144,461 | 22 | | |
| | Total | 3,303,856 | | | |
| 40–60 age | Between groups | 110,692 | 36,897 | 1,597** | 0.01 |
| | Within groups | 1,389,072 | 23 | | |
| | Total | 1,499,764 | | | |

*Note* Dependent Variable—Average Years of Completed Education; Categorical variable used for ANOVA is *Social Group*; ** indicates significance at 1 % level

**Table 6** Educational disparity—standard errors from Games-Howell post-hoc test

| Social group pairs | Parents | Children | 20–40 age | 40–60 age |
|---|---|---|---|---|
| General versus scheduled tribe | 0.043** | 0.043** | 0.043** | 0.043** |
| General versus scheduled caste | 0.043** | 0.043** | 0.043** | 0.043** |
| General versus OBC | 0.043** | 0.043** | 0.043** | 0.043** |
| OBC versus scheduled tribe | 0.042** | 0.042** | 0.042** | 0.042** |
| OBC versus scheduled caste | 0.042** | 0.042** | 0.042** | 0.042** |
| Scheduled caste versus scheduled tribe | 0.047** | 0.047** | 0.047** | 0.047** |

*Note* Variable—Average Years of Completed Education; ** indicates significance at 1 % level

## *Occupational Disparity*

Occupation levels are categories themselves and hence are not amenable to *t* test or ANOVA. Therefore to statistically examine whether occupational pattern varies significantly across social groups we have used two different procedures—the Segregation Index, and the Cross-tabulation.

The Segregation Index is commonly used for measuring inter-group differences in occupational pattern and is given by

$$D = \frac{1}{2}\sum_{i} |p_{i1} - p_{i2}|; \tag{1}$$

where $p_{i1}$ and $p_{i2}$ are proportion of Group-1 and Group-2 workers respectively in the *i*th occupation, assuming that the second group is notionally the disadvantaged group. If there are k occupational groups, then D will vary between 0, indicating perfect similarity between the two groups, to (k/2) for perfect mismatch between them. D can thereafter be normalised by dividing by k/2 so as to lie between 0 and 1. This normalised value of D (or *d*) is reported here. We have computed *d* for the SCs, STs, and the OBCs separately, each with the General/Advanced Class as the reference group.

It is observed that the occupational patterns of the disadvantaged classes are significantly different from that of the advanced class, as indicated by values of the normalised segregation index (Table 7). Segregation Index for the SCs and the OBCs are lower for the current generation (*children*) and the 20–40 age cohort compared to the previous generation (*parents*) and the 40+ age cohort, indicating that occupational pattern of these two social groups are coming nearer to that of

**Table 7** Occupational disparity—segregation index and cross-tabulation results

| Groups | Social group | d (Normalised segregation index) | Cross-tabulation results | |
|---|---|---|---|---|
| | | | Chi square | Likelihood ratio |
| Parents | Scheduled tribe | 0.22 | 7,611.5** | 7,578.6** |
| | Scheduled caste | 0.22 | | |
| | Other backward classes | 0.15 | | |
| Children | Scheduled tribe | 0.31 | 4,466.9** | 4,381.5** |
| | Scheduled caste | 0.20 | | |
| | Other backward classes | 0.14 | | |
| 20–40 age | Scheduled tribe | 0.27 | 7,741.8** | 7,609.3** |
| | Scheduled caste | 0.20 | | |
| | Other backward classes | 0.14 | | |
| 40–60 age | Scheduled tribe | 0.22 | 3,783.7** | 3,784.2** |
| | Scheduled caste | 0.24 | | |
| | Other backward classes | 0.17 | | |

*Note* Segregation index calculated with reference to the general/advanced group; ** indicates significance at 1 % level

the general/advanced class over generation and time. However, for the STs, measure of segregation has increased, indicating that workers of this social group have remained concentrated in their traditional occupations, thereby increasing the disparity with the others. This is an early indication of slow occupational mobility of the STs.

We have also cross-tabulated occupational groups with social groups and computed cell frequencies. This provides us with the standard tests of association between the two qualitative variables—the Chi square test and the Likelihood Ratio test. Results indicate that strong association exists between social group and occupational group as all the coefficients are statistically significant.

Results therefore suggest that there is systematic difference between the social groups in terms of occupational pattern and caste-membership is an important factor in determining occupational groups of individuals.

## Summary Observations

It thus transpires that in India two crucial aspects of livelihood—education and labour market—have witnessed disparity across social groups based on caste. There are signs of continuity and stagnation rather than dynamic changes and social hierarchy along caste lines have remained more or less unchanged, even being reinforced on occasions, creating wide divide between the lagging social classes and the advanced classes. Whether this is due to intergenerational transmission of human capabilities and occupational choice will be our main enquiry in the following chapters.

# Intergenerational Mobility

## The Mobility Matrix Approach

Disparities in education and occupational status among various social classes have been a reality in India. We are however more interested in examining how children's education and occupation are related to parental standards. More specifically we want to quantify the degree of intergenerational upward mobility in education and occupation. In the literature this has been done using the Mobility Matrix or cross-tabulation of children's parameters with parental parameters. Thereafter, the percentage of children moving to a higher educational or occupational class compared to their parents provides us a measure of intergenerational mobility.

Data (unit-level records) from two quinquennal surveys on employment and unemployment conducted by India's National Sample Survey Organisation (NSSO) for the 50th and the 61st rounds, pertaining to 1993 and 2004, have been used. The NSSO data provides a volume of information for each individual in the sample, of which those of interest to us are age, gender, educational level, work status, occupational group if working, wages received, etc., along with household characteristics like social group (caste), religion, location of residence, and monthly per capita expenditure. Educational levels are provided as broad groups while occupational groups follow the National Occupational Classification of 1968. For all individuals it also provides information on relation with head of household. Based on this information we can identify three different sets of parents-children from the dataset—the head of household/their spouse and their children; head of household/their brothers/sisters and their parents; sons/daughters of head of household/their spouses and grandchildren of the head of household. Using household serial numbers and person serial numbers from the dataset, comprehensive records with characteristics of two generations were prepared and family/household particulars were superimposed on them.[1] The three different sets of parent-children matches were pooled together to form the final dataset.

[1] This required use of modern econometric and database software like SPSS (student version) and Visual FoxPro Version-9. Latter econometric exercises also took help of these programmes as also Microsoft Office suite. SPSS syntax may be available from the author on request.


DOI: 10.1007/978-81-322-1130-3_3, 

This resulted in households being counted once or more, depending on whether it contains more than one set of parent-children match. Since our focus is on two successive generations, households are not the unit of study, and so counting a household more than once is not problematic. The only purpose of the household information is to enable us to identify the parent-children match and the social class to which they belong. Thus our data provides us necessary information on education and occupation for two generations along with household characteristics and can be summarised separately for different castes, age groups, gender, and location. The first generation is called *parents* and is divided into *fathers* and *mothers* while the second generation is called *children* and are subdivided into *sons* and *daughters*. Only persons aged 20 or above have been included in our study to allow them to complete the full educational cycle. Moreover, the older age-groups, even if belonging to the *children's* generation are more likely to exhibit the legacy of a distant past. To address this issue, we divide the individuals into 10-year cohorts—20–30 years of age, 31–40 years, 41–50 years, 51–60 years, and those above 60. While results for the whole sample are reported, results for the two youngest cohorts should be representative of recent trends in society. Since the NSSO database also provides multipliers to convert sample characteristics into population characteristics, we report population estimates in our study.

A note on the limitations of the database seems necessary at this point. Imposition of the age-restriction truncates the data and we are left with a smaller sample than the actual NSSO coverage and such truncation may not be non-random. Second, since the NSSO sample uses the household as the sampling frame, and as we are using household-level information to generate our dataset, we are including only those households with at least two generations living in the same household. This excludes a large number of women who have been married and have left their parents' household. The results for girls/daughters therefore have to be taken with a bit of caution. However, since our main objective is to bring out the differences between different castes, assuming that sample elimination is similarly distributed across castes, we can continue our analysis without much of a problem.

## Educational Mobility

It is observed that a substantial upward mobility across generations is present in terms of educational attainment levels (Fig. 1). About 48 % of children in 1993 and about 56 % of children in 2004 have higher educational levels compared to their parents (Tables 1 and 2). Mobility is higher for the younger age group compared to the older, and for boys compared to girls. Mobility has also improved during 1993–2004, especially for the girls.

However, social disparity in mobility levels is quite glaring. Upward mobility was quite lower for the excluded castes compared to the advanced castes in 1993. The gap has decreased in 2004, especially for the boys, but is still significant. It is

**Table 1** Upward educational mobility of different generations in India—1993 (%)

| Social group | All age group | | | 20–40 age group | | | 40+ age group | | |
|---|---|---|---|---|---|---|---|---|---|
| | Boys | Girls | All | Boys | Girls | All | Boys | Girls | All |
| Scheduled tribe | 47.5 | 18.1 | 35.2 | 47.9 | 18.4 | 35.5 | 34.2 | 3.8 | 24.3 |
| Scheduled caste | 54.6 | 23.3 | 42.3 | 54.9 | 23.6 | 42.7 | 40.3 | 16.1 | 30.0 |
| Other backward classes | na | na | na | na | na | na | na | na | na |
| General/advanced class | 62.0 | 35.9 | 51.3 | 61.9 | 36.5 | 51.5 | 66.7 | 17.0 | 47.6 |
| Aggregate | 59.8 | 32.7 | 48.8 | 59.8 | 33.3 | 49.0 | 62.3 | 16.2 | 44.5 |

*Source* Author's calculations based on data sources mentioned in the text

**Table 2** Upward educational mobility of different generations in India—2004 (%)

| Social group | All age group | | | 20–40 age group | | | 40+ age group | | |
|---|---|---|---|---|---|---|---|---|---|
| | Boys | Girls | All | Boys | Girls | All | Boys | Girls | All |
| Scheduled tribe | 60.6 | 36.4 | 51.1 | 61.4 | 36.6 | 51.5 | 42.3 | 25.7 | 39.0 |
| Scheduled caste | 64.2 | 37.7 | 54.0 | 64.5 | 38.2 | 54.2 | 57.2 | 13.6 | 47.7 |
| Other backward classes | 66.4 | 41.6 | 56.3 | 66.3 | 42.0 | 56.2 | 68.4 | 31.7 | 59.2 |
| General/advanced class | 63.1 | 50.4 | 58.0 | 62.8 | 50.6 | 57.8 | 69.2 | 45.9 | 63.1 |
| Aggregate | 64.4 | 43.7 | 56.1 | 64.4 | 44.0 | 56.1 | 65.7 | 35.5 | 58.2 |

*Source* Author's calculations based on data sources mentioned in the text

also observed that for new male entrants, probability of reaching a higher educational standard than their parents is almost equal for the advanced and excluded castes. This is a welcome trend, though the gender bias is still a major issue.

## Occupational Mobility

Compared to Educational mobility, occupational attainment is much more sticky across generations with upward mobility being only about 13–18 % in 1993, and 15–19 % in 2004 (Tables 3 and 4). Mobility has improved during 1993–2004 for all the sub-groups. At detailed occupational level, only about one-fifth of the boys

**Table 3** Upward occupational mobility of different generations in India—1993 (%)

| Social group | All age group | | | 20–40 age group | | | 40+ age group | | |
|---|---|---|---|---|---|---|---|---|---|
| | Boys | Girls | All | Boys | Girls | All | Boys | Girls | All |
| Scheduled tribe | 7.0 | 9.0 | 7.6 | 7.0 | 9.1 | 7.7 | 2.5 | 0.0 | 1.8 |
| Scheduled caste | 12.6 | 16.8 | 13.5 | 12.6 | 16.9 | 13.4 | 18.7 | 18.0 | 18.5 |
| Other backward classes | na | na | na | na | na | na | na | na | na |
| General/advanced class | 13.7 | 13.2 | 13.6 | 13.6 | 13.2 | 13.5 | 19.1 | 14.8 | 18.3 |
| Aggregate | 12.9 | 13.1 | 13.0 | 12.9 | 13.1 | 12.9 | 18.0 | 13.8 | 17.1 |

*Source* Author's calculations based on data sources mentioned in the text

**Table 4** Upward occupational mobility of different generations in India—2004 (%)

| Social group | All age group | | | 20–40 age group | | | 40+ age group | | |
|---|---|---|---|---|---|---|---|---|---|
| | Boys | Girls | All | Boys | Girls | All | Boys | Girls | All |
| Scheduled tribe | 16.6 | 8.7 | 9.7 | 10.1 | 8.8 | 9.7 | 14.3 | 2.3 | 11.2 |
| Scheduled caste | 20.8 | 18.0 | 15.7 | 14.9 | 18.1 | 15.5 | 29.1 | 12.9 | 25.9 |
| Other backward classes | 18.1 | 12.6 | 14.7 | 15.2 | 12.8 | 14.7 | 18.1 | 3.4 | 15.3 |
| General/advanced class | 20.9 | 20.4 | 17.4 | 16.7 | 20.6 | 17.4 | 20.0 | 11.3 | 18.7 |
| Aggregate | 19.3 | 15.1 | 15.3 | 15.2 | 15.3 | 15.2 | 19.9 | 7.1 | 17.6 |

*Source* Author's calculations based on data sources mentioned in the text

and one-seventh of the girls are moving to higher level of jobs compared to their parents (Fig. 2). For the advanced castes however, mobility among girls is higher compared to boys, indicating wider acceptability of upper caste women in diversified occupational positions and also higher aspirations among present generation women of the advanced castes. However, much of this mobility is perceived to be at comparable hierarchical level and grade level stickiness is observed to be much higher when viewed at broad occupational levels. Only about one-tenth of workers in 2004 have better occupational grades compared to their parents (Tables 5 and 6).

Mobility among excluded castes is lower than that for advanced castes indicating greater intergenerational stickiness for the former. This gap is higher at broad occupational levels compared to detailed occupational levels. Thus, it emerges that for the advanced castes, the mobility from Blue Collar to Pink Collar and from Pink

**Table 5** Upward occupational mobility (broad group) of different generations in India—1993

| Social group | All age group | | | 20–40 age group | | | 40+ age group | | |
|---|---|---|---|---|---|---|---|---|---|
| | Boys | Girls | All | Boys | Girls | All | Boys | Girls | All |
| Scheduled tribe | 5.0 | 6.4 | 5.4 | 5.1 | 6.5 | 5.5 | 2.5 | 0.0 | 1.8 |
| Scheduled caste | 8.0 | 8.7 | 8.1 | 7.9 | 8.7 | 8.1 | 17.1 | 7.5 | 14.4 |
| Other backward classes | na | na | na | na | na | na | na | na | na |
| General/advanced class | 10.7 | 9.2 | 10.5 | 10.6 | 9.2 | 10.3 | 18.0 | 12.3 | 16.9 |
| Aggregate | 9.8 | 8.7 | 9.6 | 9.7 | 8.7 | 9.5 | 16.9 | 10.3 | 15.6 |

*Source* Author's calculations based on data sources mentioned in the text

**Table 6** Upward occupational mobility (broad group) of different generations in India—2004

| Social group | All age group | | | 20–40 age group | | | 40+ age group | | |
|---|---|---|---|---|---|---|---|---|---|
| | Boys | Girls | All | Boys | Girls | All | Boys | Girls | All |
| Scheduled tribe | 7.7 | 4.5 | 6.8 | 7.6 | 4.6 | 6.8 | 14.0 | 2.3 | 11.0 |
| Scheduled caste | 10.2 | 7.2 | 9.7 | 10.0 | 7.1 | 9.4 | 27.7 | 11.7 | 24.5 |
| Other backward classes | 12.1 | 8.3 | 11.3 | 12.0 | 8.5 | 11.3 | 15.7 | 3.4 | 13.4 |
| General/advanced class | 13.5 | 15.6 | 13.9 | 13.4 | 15.9 | 13.8 | 16.7 | 5.8 | 15.0 |
| Aggregate | 11.9 | 9.6 | 11.4 | 11.7 | 9.7 | 11.3 | 17.3 | 5.1 | 15.1 |

*Source* Author's calculations based on data sources mentioned in the text

Collar to White Collar jobs is existent while for the excluded castes much of the mobility is lateral, i.e. from one occupation to other within the same broad grade.

Quite surprisingly, mobility is higher among older age group people compared to the young. This may be due to various reasons. First, this may be a reflection of lower initial or parental occupational levels of the current 40+ people compared to the current 20–40 age group people whose parents have already higher occupational levels. Hence upward mobility may be higher for the former compared to the latter. Second, this may also be because of tighter labour market situations in recent times whereby chances of vertical mobility have become much sparser and most of the movements are horizontal among similar occupations. Overall educational and occupational mobility picture is represented in Fig. 3.

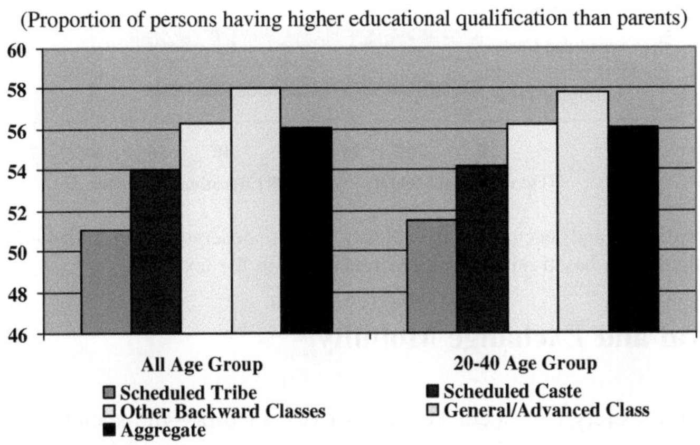


**Fig. 1** Educational mobility across generations in India—2004. *Source* Author's calculations based on data sources mentioned in the text

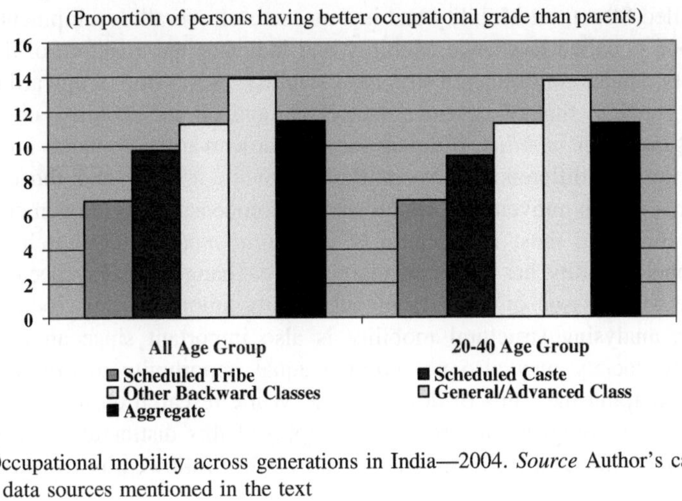


**Fig. 2** Occupational mobility across generations in India—2004. *Source* Author's calculations based on data sources mentioned in the text

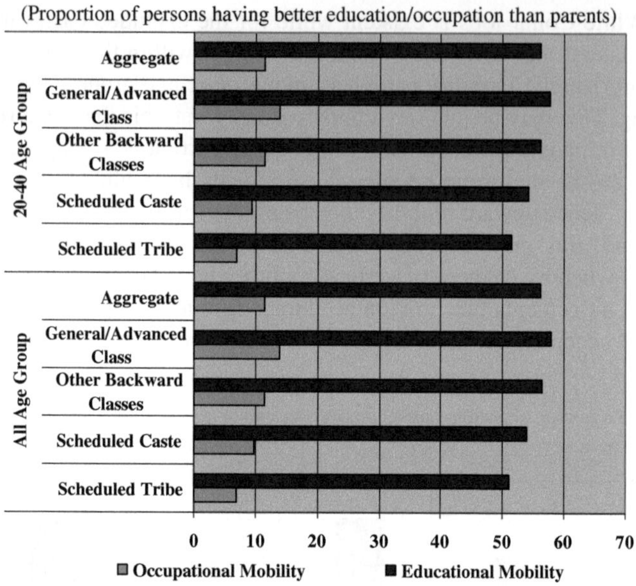


**Fig. 3** Educational and occupational mobility across generations in India—2004. *Source* Author's calculations based on data sources mentioned in the text

## Structural and Exchange Mobility

Mobility in a society can occur because of two factors—the society may develop and expand over time providing better and more opportunities to the future generation than the present one; or/and there may occur social churning whereby some people improving upon their parental background at the cost of some people going down while the aggregate opportunities in the society remains unchanged. The first one is called Structural Mobility and is a measure of overall development and the second one is called Exchange Mobility and indicates the quantum of fluidity in the society. Under conditions of structural stability, proportion of upward mobility must be equal to that of downward mobility and all the mobility observed in society is *exchange mobility*. If the upward and downward movements are unequal in size, the net difference between those moving upward and those moving downward—that is movements which are not compensated by movements in the opposite direction, must be because of *structural mobility*. Research on intergenerational mobility has focussed mainly on exchange mobility because of its relevance to the issue of equality of opportunity among various social classes. However, analysing structural mobility is also important since an expanding/developing society may also not provide equal opportunity to different social classes in reaping the fruits of development. While research on intergenerational mobility by sociologists has frequently employed this distinction in explaining observed mobility data [starting with Rogoff (1953), followed by Duncan (1966);

Featherman et al. (1975); Goldthorpe (1980); Hope (1982); Hauser and Grusky (1988) and Sobel et al. (1998)], economists have been sluggish in fully appraising and utilizing the distinction between structural and exchange mobility in their studies. We have attempted in decomposing the observed mobility for the 2004 data into *structural* and *exchange* mobility and examining the pattern.

## Components of Educational Mobility

We find that there is a clear gender distinction regarding relative importance of structural and exchange mobility in educational levels (Tables 7 and 8). For the males (boys) most of the observed mobility is due to structural factors and only a small part (about one-seventh) is due to exchange mobility. For females however, structural and exchange mobility are quite close in magnitude though in this case too structural factors seem to be dominating. Structural mobility is higher for males compared to females—more than double in most cases. Improved and expanded educational system appears to have benefitted the boy child much more compared to the girl child, indicating intra-household gender discrimination. On the other hand exchange mobility is higher for females compared to males signaling that social fluidity is more and parental inertia is less for the girls. We also find that in the previous decade (1993 data, tables suppressed) disparity between the advanced social class and the lagging classes were substantial for both structural and exchange mobility. In the later decade however, the gap between social classes in terms of structural mobility has narrowed down, though exchange mobility for the lagging classes are still way below that of the advanced class. This indicates that new opportunities that have come up in recent times have benefitted various classes almost similarly.

## Components of Occupational Mobility

Decomposing occupational mobility data into structural and exchange components throw up certain interesting results (Tables 9 and 10). For the advanced class and

**Table 7** Upward structural mobility in India—education—2004

| Social group | All age group | | | 20–40 age group | | | 40+ age group | | |
|---|---|---|---|---|---|---|---|---|---|
| | Boys | Girls | All | Boys | Girls | All | Boys | Girls | All |
| Scheduled tribe | 54.1 | 21.4 | 41.2 | 55.0 | 21.4 | 41.5 | 36.2 | 24.0 | 33.6 |
| Scheduled caste | 56.7 | 21.8 | 43.2 | 56.7 | 22.4 | 43.3 | 55.6 | 7.7 | 42.6 |
| Other backward classes | 57.4 | 21.7 | 42.6 | 57.1 | 22.1 | 42.4 | 63.0 | 15.5 | 50.8 |
| General/advanced class | 51.8 | 31.7 | 43.7 | 51.1 | 32.3 | 43.4 | 63.1 | 26.4 | 52.2 |
| Aggregate | 55.0 | 24.9 | 42.9 | 54.8 | 25.4 | 42.8 | 60.4 | 16.7 | 49.3 |

*Source* Author's calculations based on data sources mentioned in the text

**Table 8** Upward exchange mobility in India—education—2004

| Social group | All age group | | | 20–40 age group | | | 40+ age group | | |
|---|---|---|---|---|---|---|---|---|---|
| | Boys | Girls | All | Boys | Girls | All | Boys | Girls | All |
| Scheduled tribe | 6.5 | 15.0 | 9.9 | 6.4 | 15.2 | 10.0 | 6.1 | 1.7 | 5.4 |
| Scheduled caste | 7.5 | 15.9 | 10.8 | 7.8 | 15.8 | 10.9 | 1.6 | 5.9 | 5.1 |
| Other backward classes | 9.0 | 19.9 | 13.7 | 9.2 | 19.9 | 13.8 | 5.4 | 16.2 | 8.4 |
| General/advanced class | 11.3 | 18.7 | 14.3 | 11.7 | 18.3 | 14.4 | 6.1 | 19.5 | 10.9 |
| Aggregate | 9.4 | 18.8 | 13.2 | 9.6 | 18.6 | 13.3 | 5.3 | 18.8 | 8.9 |

*Source* Author's calculations based on data sources mentioned in the text

also for the OBCs, exchange mobility and structural mobility are almost equal in magnitude. However, in case of the two bottom-most categories, STs and SCs, structural mobility is twice that of exchange mobility for the males while for the females exchange mobility is higher. This also translates to the fact that structural mobility rates of males are higher than females while the opposite is true for exchange mobility. This again indicates that emergence of new occupational opportunities in the society/economy has benefitted the males much more than the females, social fluidity and exchange of places being more pronounced for the latter. As with education, structural mobility is almost similar across social classes while exchange mobility is definitely higher for the advanced class compared to the lagging classes.

It therefore emerges from our decomposing observed mobility data into structural and exchange factors that there are clear distinctions between males and

**Table 9** Upward structural mobility in India—occupation—2004

| Social group | All age group | | | 20–40 age group | | | 40+ age group | | |
|---|---|---|---|---|---|---|---|---|---|
| | Boys | Girls | All | Boys | Girls | All | Boys | Girls | All |
| Scheduled tribe | 12.0 | 4.0 | 6.1 | 7.3 | 3.9 | 6.1 | 13.5 | 2.3 | 11.0 |
| Scheduled caste | 12.3 | 6.5 | 7.2 | 8.8 | 6.6 | 7.1 | 26.6 | 12.9 | 23.4 |
| Other backward classes | 9.4 | 6.0 | 7.1 | 7.9 | 6.1 | 7.1 | 10.9 | 3.4 | 8.6 |
| General/advanced class | 10.5 | 10.6 | 7.9 | 8.5 | 10.5 | 7.9 | 13.2 | 9.9 | 12.4 |
| Aggregate | 10.1 | 4.9 | 7.0 | 8.0 | 5.0 | 7.0 | 12.9 | 6.6 | 11.0 |

*Source* Author's calculations based on data sources mentioned in the text

**Table 10** Upward exchange mobility in India—occupation—2004

| Social group | All age group | | | 20–40 age group | | | 40+ age group | | |
|---|---|---|---|---|---|---|---|---|---|
| | Boys | Girls | All | Boys | Girls | All | Boys | Girls | All |
| Scheduled tribe | 4.6 | 4.7 | 3.6 | 2.8 | 4.9 | 3.6 | 0.8 | 0.0 | 0.2 |
| Scheduled caste | 8.5 | 11.5 | 8.5 | 6.1 | 11.5 | 8.4 | 2.5 | 0.0 | 2.5 |
| Other backward classes | 8.7 | 6.6 | 7.6 | 7.3 | 6.7 | 7.6 | 7.2 | 0.0 | 6.7 |
| General/advanced class | 10.4 | 9.8 | 9.5 | 8.2 | 10.1 | 9.5 | 6.8 | 1.4 | 6.3 |
| Aggregate | 9.2 | 10.2 | 8.3 | 7.2 | 10.3 | 8.2 | 7.0 | 0.5 | 6.6 |

*Source* Author's calculations based on data sources mentioned in the text

females in terms of relative importance of the two components. For males, general advancement of society and opening up of new educational and occupational vistas has been the driving force behind upward movement across generations. For the females, social fluidity and exchange of places have been more important rather than partaking in the new opportunities. Moreover, the structural advancement seems to have benefitted all the social classes almost similarly while exchange mobility is certainly lower for the lagging social classes, especially the STs, creating a polarizing trend in social hierarchy.

## Summary Observations

This section aimed at exploring the intergenerational mobility in educational and occupational status of different castes in India, especially the quantum of upward mobility exhibited by these groups, and examining whether inter-group disparities in mobility are significant. Four issues emerge from our results. First, educational and occupational structure and hierarchy have remained biased in favour of the *Advanced Castes* even after 60 years of our independence and a string of affirmative action, though the current generations are better off compared to their parents. Second, such upward mobility is pronounced for the *Advanced Castes* while the parental influence is much stronger for the *Excluded Castes*. Hence intergenerational mobility is significantly lower for the latter compared to the former. Third, occupational mobility is lower than educational mobility and may be a sign of discrimination in the labour market. Fourth, much of the occupational movement is within broad occupational grades and movement from Blue-Collar to Pink-Collar or to White-Collar jobs are not substantial, especially for the *Excluded Castes*.

## References

Featheman DL, Jones FL, Hauser RM (1975) Assumptions of Mobility Research: The Case of Occupational Status. Soc Sci Res 4:329–360

Goldthorpe JH (1980) Social Mobility and Class Structure in Modern Britain. Clarendon Press. Oxford

Hope K (1982) Vertical and Nonvertical Class Mobility in Three Countries. Amer Sociol Rev 47:99–113

Hauser RM, Grusky DB (1988) Cross National Variation in Occupational Distributions, Relative Mobility Chances, and Intergenerational Shifts in Occupational Distributions. Amer Sociol Rev 53:723–741

Duncan O (1966) Methodological Issues in the Analysis of Economic Mobility in Social Structure and Mobility in Economic Development, ed. by Smelser N and Lipset S. Aldine, Chicago: 51–97

Rogoff N (1953) Recent Trends in Occupational Mobility. The Free Press, Glencoe

Sobel ME, Becker MP, Minick SM (1988) Origins, destinations, and association in occupational mobility. Amer Sociol Rev 104:687–721

# Inertia Across Generations

## A Multivariate Approach

In the previous section we have reported the proportion of current generation individuals achieving higher educational and occupational level compared to their parents, separately for different castes and gender in India. Such upward movement is observed to be lower for the excluded castes compared to the advanced castes. But is such stickiness really due to the caste factor or are other factors responsible? For example, one factor that promptly seems to be important is the economic condition of the family. To answer this, we have applied a Multivariate Regression Method where the *Children*'s characteristics have been regressed on *Parental* characteristics along with other explanatory variables. In this chapter we will explore the results from such a multivariate econometric exercise involving the most recent dataset pertaining to 2004.

## Methodology

The regression function that fits our objective can be specified as:

$$\begin{aligned} C_i = \alpha + \beta F_i + \gamma M_i + \theta\,(\text{Social Group Dummies}) + \varphi\,(\text{Poverty Status}) \\ + \lambda\,(\text{Cohort Effects}) + \text{error term} \end{aligned} \quad (1)$$

$C_i$ is ith Child's characteristic related to education/occupation;
$F_i$ and $M_i$ are ith child's Father's and Mother's characteristic related to education/occupation;

The coefficients $\beta$ and $\gamma$ relate the education/occupation level of children to that of their parents. A higher value for these coefficients implies stronger parental effects on the children, higher intergenerational stickiness, and therefore less mobility. $\theta$ denotes base level difference between social groups regarding educational/occupational achievements. Effect of household income is captured by Poverty Status, which is a Dummy Variable taking value 1 if the MPCE of the household is less than the Poverty Line, and thus $\varphi$ signifies how poverty status

R. Majumder, *Intergenerational Mobility*, SpringerBriefs in Economics, DOI: 10.1007/978-81-322-1130-3_4, © The Author(s) 2013

affects achievement levels.[1] $\lambda$ will measure base level differences among different age cohorts regarding educational/occupational achievements. To examine differences between different castes or gender regarding parental influence two approaches can be taken.

First, Eq. (1) can be collapsed to:

$$C_i = \alpha + \beta F_i + \gamma M_i + \varphi\,(\text{Poverty Status}) + \text{ error term} \tag{2}$$

This equation can now be estimated separately for different location/caste/gender/cohort groups and the values of $\beta$ and $\gamma$ can be compared across those groups. Higher $\beta$ and $\gamma$ for *Excluded Castes* and *Females* would indicate greater inertia and lower mobility for them.

In the second approach, Eq. (1) can be expanded to:

$$\begin{aligned} C_i &= \alpha + \beta F_i + \gamma M_i + j\,(Poverty\,Status) + \theta\,(Social\,Group\,Dummies) \\ &\quad + \theta'(Interaction\,Dummies\,of\,Social\,Groups\,with\,Parental\,characteristics) \\ &\quad + error\,term \end{aligned} \tag{3}$$

Estimates of $\theta'$ would provide us measures of differential parental impact for different castes. Equation (3) may again be estimated separately for location, gender and cohort groups. A positive $\theta'$ will indicate higher parental impact for *Excluded Castes.*

In addition to this regression technique, one can also use Partial Correlation method to measure the association between parental and child's characteristic after controlling for variables like Poverty status etc. A higher correlation coefficient would imply substantial intergenerational inertia.

We have used both the regression methods as well as the correlation method to examine the issue of intergenerational transmission of educational and occupational characteristics in India.

## Parental Impact on Education

To explore inertia in educational achievements, we have used Completed Years of Education as the characteristic variable.[2] Since education of both parents and children are now measured in numbers of years of schooling, the coefficients

[1] MPCE—Monthly Per-capita Consumption Expenditure is a proxy of income/consumption status in India. Poverty Line refers to the monetary approximation of calorific norms of poverty. For details see http://planningcommission.nic.in/reports/genrep/rep_pov.pdf.

[2] Completed Years of Education are derived from the Educational Status of individuals. As per Indian educational structure, following values were arrived at: —Illiterate = 0, Literate but below Primary level education = 3, Primary School (Class 5) Passed = 5, Middle School (Class 8) Passed = 8, Secondary School (Class 10) Passed = 10, Higher Secondary (Class 12) Passed = 12, Graduate and above = 15.

would measure how much difference in the schooling of children is caused by a difference of 1 year in the father's/mother's schooling. Results indicate that for the rural areas Parental educational levels have significant impact on the children's educational level (Table 1). Notably, for the *Daughters*, impact of maternal education is stronger than that of the father. Also, this maternal impact is stronger for daughters compared to that for sons. This indicates the importance of women's education in sending the girl child to school. As expected, the parental impacts are lower for the younger cohorts indicating decline in intergenerational inertia in educational achievements over time. The intercepts for the *Excluded Castes* are significantly lower indicating lower average educational achievements for them compared to the upper castes. Poverty also significantly lowers educational attainment of individuals.

Our main interest however is to examine whether parental impacts are systematically higher for *Excluded Castes* compared to others. This would be revealed by the difference among castes regarding the values of coefficients $\beta$ and $\gamma$ in Eq. (2) or by the value of the coefficients of the slope dummies ($\theta'$) of Eq. (3). It is observed that Father's education have significantly greater impact for all the three *Excluded Castes* compared to the upper castes—supporting our hypothesis that intergenerational mobility is lower for these groups (Table 2). Impact of maternal education is also greater for these groups, though the coefficients are significant only at 20 % level. The results hold for both the functional forms used.

For the Urban areas, the broad trends of the results are similar, though now fewer coefficients are significant (Table 3). Interestingly, for the SCs and STs in urban areas, the impact of father's education is more important for the boys while for the girls, mother's education is more important. Moreover, stickiness is more pronounced for the girls compared to the boys.

Another observation is that for the urban population cohort effects are much less pronounced with very little difference between the various age groups in terms of the degree of stickiness (Table 4).

As noted earlier, the coefficients of parental educational levels in Eqs. (2) and (3) are measures of intergenerational stickiness and therefore their inverse can be taken as a measure of intergenerational mobility. These Mobility Indices are reported in Table 5 for both the equations. It is observed that mobility is substantially lower for the *Excluded Castes* compared to the upper castes, and also for the *Daughters* compared to the *Sons*. Thus, even after allowing for differences in income level (proxied by MPCE) mobility is lower for the excluded groups. If we consider the fact that poverty itself is much higher among the *Excluded Castes*, and poverty puts a downward pressure on educational attainment, these groups are thus doubly disadvantaged.

**Table 1** Determinants of years of schooling in India—2004—RURAL

| Dep var—comp years of school (Meth: sep regr) | Scheduled tribe | | Scheduled caste | | OBC | | General | |
|---|---|---|---|---|---|---|---|---|
| | Boys | Girls | Boys | Girls | Boys | Girls | Boys | Girls |
| (Constant) | 5.824 | 5.924 | 6.312 | 6.595 | 7.275 | 6.892 | 7.144 | 7.568 |
| | (68.5)** | (68.1)** | (117.3)** | (116.4)** | (30.9)** | (41.6)** | (74.6)** | (93.4)** |
| Father's education | 0.413 | 0.410 | 0.387 | 0.357 | 0.312 | 0.340 | 0.349 | 0.348 |
| | (22.6)** | (22.7)** | (39.1)** | (37.5)** | (9.4)** | (14.9)** | (26.6)** | (33.1)** |
| Mother's education | 0.170 | 0.176 | 0.168 | 0.180 | 0.066 | 0.137 | 0.139 | 0.108 |
| | (4.3)** | (5.2)** | (11.0)** | (13.7)** | (1.8)** | (4.2)** | (8.8)** | (10.1)** |
| Poverty status | −1.994 | −1.467 | −1.402 | −1.355 | −1.673 | −1.773 | −1.473 | −2.025 |
| | (13.4)** | (10.1)** | (14.7)** | (11.5)** | (5.3)** | (9.5)** | (13.8)** | (20.1)** |
| *Adjusted R squared* | *0.26* | *0.21* | *0.24* | *0.27* | *0.31* | *0.30* | *0.33* | *0.39* |

*Source* Author's calculations based on Data Sources mentioned in the text
*Note* Figures in parenthesis are *t*-values. * and ** indicates significance at 1 and 5 % levels respectively

**Table 2** Determinants of years of schooling in India—2004—RURAL

| Dep var—comp years of school (Meth: dummy) | All ages | | 20–30 age group | | 30–40 age group | |
|---|---|---|---|---|---|---|
| | Boys | Girls | Boys | Girls | Boys | Girls |
| (Constant) | 6.979 (106.6)** | 4.933 (60.3)** | 7.006 (91.8)** | 5.249 (57.0)** | 6.947 (48.9)** | 4.059 (21.6)** |
| Father's education | 0.347 (31.0)** | 0.307 (22.4)** | 0.331 (26.1)** | 0.315 (20.8)** | 0.386 (14.9)** | 0.254 (7.4)** |
| Mother's education | 0.154 (10.1)** | 0.360 (19.4)** | 0.149 (8.9)** | 0.318 (15.9)** | 0.196 (5.1)** | 0.522 (9.5)** |
| Scheduled tribe dummy | −1.453 (14.4)** | −1.881 (14.9)** | −1.480 (12.8)** | −2.102 (15.1)** | −1.455 (6.2)** | −1.565 (4.9)** |
| Scheduled caste dummy | −1.072 (11.3)** | −1.519 (12.4)** | −1.177 (11.0)** | −1.701 (12.7)** | −0.629 (2.7)** | −1.155 (3.7)** |
| OBC dummy | −0.522 (6.7)** | −1.103 (11.6)** | −0.541 (6.1)** | −1.149 (10.8)** | −0.439 (2.5)** | −1.213 (5.4)** |
| ST dummy * Father's education | 0.121 (5.3)** | 0.090 (3.2)** | 0.120 (4.8)** | 0.079 (2.6)** | 0.151 (2.4)** | 0.133 (1.5) |
| SC dummy * Father's education | 0.170 (3.5)** | 0.182 (3.2)** | 0.183 (3.8)** | 0.178 (2.9)** | 0.144 (0.7) | 0.143 (0.5) |
| OBC dummy * Father's education | 0.033 (2.3)** | 0.011 (0.6) | 0.034 (2.1)** | 0.037 (1.9)** | 0.036 (1.0) | 0.120 (2.6)** |
| ST dummy * Mother's education | 0.057 (1.7)* | 0.027 (0.6) | 0.042 (1.1) | 0.020 (0.4) | 0.093 (0.9) | 0.090 (0.6) |
| SC dummy * Mother's education | 0.019 (0.5) | 0.051 (1.2) | 0.033 (0.9) | 0.068 (1.5) | 0.091 (0.8) | 0.257 (1.3) |
| OBC dummy * Mother's education | 0.012 (0.6) | 0.173 (6.8)** | 0.025 (1.1) | 0.216 (8.0)** | 0.026 (0.4) | 0.046 (0.5) |
| Poverty status | −1.474 (24.4)** | −1.560 (20.8)** | −1.350 (19.9)** | −1.581 (19.5)** | −1.817 (12.7)** | −1.676 (8.4)** |
| *Adjusted R squared* | *0.27* | *0.34* | *0.28* | *0.34* | *0.26* | *0.30* |
| *No. of Obs.* | *43,890* | *8,483* | *28,236* | *6,809* | *10,596* | *5,613* |

*Source* Author's calculations based on Data Sources mentioned in the text

*Note* Figures in parenthesis are *t*-values. * and ** indicates significance at 1 and 5 % levels respectively

**Table 3** Determinants of years of schooling in India—2004—URBAN

| Dep var—comp years of school (Meth: sep regr) | Scheduled tribe | | Scheduled caste | | OBC | | General | |
|---|---|---|---|---|---|---|---|---|
| | Boys | Girls | Boys | Girls | Boys | Girls | Boys | Girls |
| (Constant) | 4.020 (41.2)** | 3.573 (32.1)** | 3.752 (55.8)** | 4.835 (63.9)** | 6.057 (22.8)** | 5.472 (22.8)** | 6.106 (46.5)** | 7.172 (64.4)** |
| Father's education | 0.379 (18.0)** | 0.385 (17.6)** | 0.299 (24.5)** | 0.305 (24.5)** | 0.269 (6.7)** | 0.366 (11.7)** | 0.299 (17.3)** | 0.291 (20.9)** |
| Mother's education | 0.310 (9.8)** | 0.408 (10.5)** | 0.540 (28.1)** | 0.383 (22.5)** | 0.274 (6.1)** | 0.258 (6.1)** | 0.307 (15.0)** | 0.214 (15.6)** |
| Poverty status | −2.362 (13.6)** | −1.694 (9.7)** | −1.617 (14.0)** | −1.670 (10.6)** | −2.223 (5.7)** | −2.303 (8.7)** | −1.870 (13.4)** | −2.437 (17.9)** |
| *Adjusted R squared* | *0.33* | *0.29* | *0.29* | *0.28* | *0.38* | *0.37* | *0.37* | *0.40* |

*Source* Author's calculations based on Data Sources mentioned in the text
*Note* Figures in parenthesis are *t*-values. * and ** indicates significance at 1 and 5 % levels respectively

**Table 4** Determinants of years of schooling in India—2004—URBAN

| Dep var—comp years of school (Meth: dummy) | All ages | | 20–30 age group | | 30–40 age group | |
|---|---|---|---|---|---|---|
| | Boys | Girls | Boys | Girls | Boys | Girls |
| (Constant) | 8.038 (87.05)** | 7.478 (60.1)** | 8.370 (71.7)** | 7.579 (55.7)** | 7.799 (41.8)** | 7.214 (22.4)** |
| Father's education | 0.327 (25.9)** | 0.283 (17.2)** | 0.330 (22.3)** | 0.280 (15.6)** | 0.334 (12.2)** | 0.301 (7.0)** |
| Mother's Education | 0.082 (6.5)** | 0.191 (11.9)** | 0.088 (6.0)** | 0.190 (10.9)** | 0.078 (2.8)** | 0.177 (4.1)** |
| Scheduled tribe dummy | −0.859 (3.8)** | −1.944 (7.0)** | −0.881 (3.4)** | −2.181 (7.0)** | −0.094 (0.1) | −0.288 (0.4) |
| Scheduled caste dummy | −1.297 (9.4)** | −2.383 (12.6)** | −0.902 (5.7)** | −2.342 (11.5)** | −2.274 (6.9)** | −2.925 (5.7)** |
| OBC dummy | −0.429 (4.0)** | −0.967 (6.7)** | −0.180 (1.4) | −0.838 (5.3)** | −0.977 (4.0)** | −1.618 (4.1)** |
| ST dummy * Father's education | 0.013 (0.3) | 0.017 (0.3) | 0.018 (0.4) | 0.042 (0.8) | 0.020 (0.2) | −0.142 (1.0) |
| SC dummy * Father's education | 0.023 (1.0) | 0.101 (3.2)** | 0.000 (0.02) | 0.100 (3.0)** | 0.096 (1.5) | 0.086 (0.7) |
| OBC dummy * Father's education | 0.001 (0.03) | 0.001 (0.05) | −0.019 (1.02) | −0.012 (0.5) | 0.056 (1.4) | 0.066 (1.1) |
| ST dummy * Mother's education | 0.040 (0.9) | 0.087 (1.6) | −0.030 (0.6) | 0.089 (1.5) | −0.134 (1.1) | 0.036 (0.2) |
| SC dummy * Mother's education | 0.057 (1.8)* | 0.082 (2.1)** | 0.052 (1.5) | 0.075 (1.8)* | 0.073 (0.8) | 0.185 (1.1) |
| OBC dummy * Mother's education | 0.033 (1.7)* | 0.093 (3.9)** | 0.043 (2.1)** | 0.105 (4.1)** | 0.000 (0.01) | −0.004 (0.05) |
| Poverty status | −1.589 (23.9)** | −1.971 (22.3)** | −1.586 (21.1)** | −1.936 (20.3)** | −1.377 (8.9)** | −2.208 (9.2)** |
| *Adjusted R squared* | *0.40* | *0.45* | *0.40* | *0.45* | *0.41* | *0.48* |
| *No. of obs.* | *22,969* | *6,746* | *14,616* | *5,396* | *5,613* | *867* |

*Source* Author's calculations based on Data Sources mentioned in the text

*Note* Figures in parenthesis are *t*-values. * and ** indicates significance at 1 and 5 % levels respectively

**Table 5** Derived mobility indices of schooling in India—2004

| Method | Location | Sch Tribe | | Sch Caste | | OBC | | General | |
|---|---|---|---|---|---|---|---|---|---|
| | | Boys | Girls | Boys | Girls | Boys | Girls | Boys | Girls |
| Equation 2 | Rural | 3.8 | 2.5 | 3.4 | 2.5 | 3.6 | 2.4 | 4.0 | 2.9 |
| | Urban | 3.9 | 3.1 | 4.2 | 3.2 | 4.1 | 3.3 | 4.4 | 4.0 |
| Equation 3 | Rural | 2.3 | 2.2 | 2.3 | 1.8 | 3.4 | 1.9 | 4.0 | 3.0 |
| | Urban | 3.9 | 2.9 | 3.5 | 2.4 | 4.2 | 3.0 | 4.9 | 4.2 |

*Source* Author's calculations based on Data Sources mentioned in the text
*Note* Mobility Indices are derived as inverse of the Average of the coefficients of Father's and Mother's educational level in respective equations (Eqs. 2 and 3)

## Occupational Group and Parental Influence

Analysing Occupational Mobility in a Multivariate framework is much more complex since we can only have some ordinal ranking of the occupation groups, as mentioned earlier. In absence of any cardinal values associated with each occupation, we can advance in either of the following ways. First, and theoretically the best approach would have been to use Multinomial-Multivariate Logit models to regress occupational group of the individual as function of parental occupation, caste, and poverty status. This however would make this publication technically much more challenging and rob much of its appeal, as also would make it longer. So we do not proceed in this direction. The second method could be to rank the occupations and use the rank values as numerical variables, followed by OLS regression of Eqs. (2) and (3). But that assumes proportional ratio relationship between different discrete categories of occupations and it would not be theoretically justified to use them in a regression analysis. Hence we take the more rudimentary third option in which, after ranking the occupations, we derive Rank Correlation coefficient between an individual's occupation status and that of their parents, after controlling for effects of poverty status and cohorts. In addition, it is expected that an individual's occupation would depend on her/his educational level. Since parental influence on education has already been established, we want to remove the effect of education from intergenerational occupational inertia. Hence education of the individual has also been included as a control variable while calculating the partial correlation coefficients. These partial correlation coefficients between *Children*'s and *Parent*'s occupational ranks were calculated separately for the different castes and gender. A high and positive association would indicate substantial influence of parental occupation on that of the children while a lower coefficient would indicate higher mobility. These coefficients and derived Mobility Indices are reported in Tables 6, 7, and 8. [It may be noted that the results could have been biased if there were significant difference among the social classes in terms of labour market participation rates. However, in Indian context, though the participation rate of the advanced class is lower than that of the lagging classes, the differences are not statistically significant.]

**Table 6** Determinants of occupational status in India—2004—RURAL

Partial correlation of child's occupation after controlling for poverty status and education

| Age cohort | Variable | Sch tribe | | Sch caste | | OBC | | General | |
|---|---|---|---|---|---|---|---|---|---|
| | | Boys | Girls | Boys | Girls | Boys | Girls | Boys | Girls |
| *1 digit NOC* | | | | | | | | | |
| All ages | Father's occupation | 0.23** | 0.19* | 0.33** | 0.14* | 0.22** | 0.11 | 0.17* | 0.13 |
| | Mother's occupation | 0.27** | 0.33** | 0.21** | 0.46** | 0.14* | 0.45** | 0.18* | 0.22* |
| 20–30 age | Father's occupation | 0.37** | 0.23** | 0.36** | 0.22* | 0.26** | 0.18* | 0.22** | 0.16 |
| | Mother's occupation | 0.23** | 0.35** | 0.22* | 0.46** | 0.17 | 0.46** | 0.13* | 0.15 |
| 30–40 age | Father's occupation | 0.21** | 0.20* | 0.29** | 0.15 | 0.15 | 0.13 | 0.17* | 0.13 |
| | Mother's occupation | 0.14* | 0.50** | 0.14* | 0.62** | 0.17* | 0.43** | 0.10 | 0.37** |
| *Broad occupational group* | | | | | | | | | |
| All ages | Father's occupation | 0.24* | 0.16* | 0.27* | 0.17* | 0.26* | 0.16 | 0.22* | 0.13 |
| | Mother's occupation | 0.28** | 0.33** | 0.23* | 0.50** | 0.19* | 0.48** | 0.20* | 0.24* |
| 20–30 age | Father's occupation | 0.27* | 0.32** | 0.30** | 0.25* | 0.31** | 0.21* | 0.27** | 0.17 |
| | Mother's occupation | 0.24* | 0.37** | 0.24* | 0.51** | 0.21* | 0.49** | 0.16 | 0.27* |
| 30–40 age | Father's occupation | 0.24** | 0.20* | 0.25** | 0.01 | 0.19* | 0.06 | 0.18* | 0.12 |
| | Mother's occupation | 0.26** | 0.44** | 0.21* | 0.62** | 0.12 | 0.45** | 0.07 | 0.30** |

*Source* Author's calculations based on Data Sources mentioned in the text
*Note* * and ** indicates significance at 1 and 5 % levels respectively

It is observed that children's occupational status is significantly influenced by parent's occupation, both for 1-digit NOC and Broad occupational grade. As expected, the association is on an average stronger for the *Excluded Castes* compared to the *Advanced Castes*, and for broad occupational grades compared to 1-digit NOC. Mobility Indices are naturally higher for the *Advanced Castes* compared to the *Excluded Castes*. The results therefore confirm our earlier finding that much of the intergenerational mobility is lateral and not vertical. It is quite disheartening to note that even after half a century the results match those obtained by Driver (1962) indicating a pathetically slow pace of social churning in India.

Two notable differences from educational mobility are that here associations are stronger for the urban population compared to rural population, and that both father's and mother's occupation have greater influence on son's occupational status rather than on the daughter's occupation, except for the upper caste girls.

**Table 7** Determinants of occupational status in India—2004—URBAN

Partial correlation of child's occupation after controlling for poverty status and education

| Age cohort | Variable | Sch tribe | | Sch caste | | OBC | | General | |
|---|---|---|---|---|---|---|---|---|---|
| | | Boys | Girls | Boys | Girls | Boys | Girls | Boys | Girls |
| *1 digit NOC* | | | | | | | | | |
| All ages | Father's occupation | 0.37** | 0.38** | 0.48** | 0.28* | 0.23* | 0.27* | 0.30* | 0.21* |
| | Mother's occupation | 0.28* | 0.60** | 0.34* | 0.40** | 0.26* | 0.50** | 0.13 | 0.25* |
| 20–30 age | Father's occupation | 0.35** | 0.44** | 0.48** | 0.17 | 0.30** | 0.24* | 0.18 | 0.14 |
| | Mother's occupation | 0.39** | 0.67** | 0.33* | 0.31* | 0.29** | 0.53** | 0.20 | 0.13 |
| 30–40 age | Father's occupation | 0.12 | 0.42** | 0.36** | 0.92** | 0.21* | 0.87** | 0.20* | 0.25* |
| | Mother's occupation | 0.25* | 0.32** | 0.49** | 0.62** | 0.35** | 0.53** | 0.13 | 0.26* |
| *Broad occupational group* | | | | | | | | | |
| All ages | Father's occupation | 0.28** | 0.41** | 0.55** | 0.41** | 0.33* | 0.39** | 0.25* | 0.29* |
| | Mother's occupation | 0.41** | 0.63** | 0.42** | 0.62** | 0.36** | 0.61** | 0.16 | 0.25 |
| 20–30 age | Father's occupation | 0.35** | 0.52** | 0.54** | 0.31* | 0.39** | 0.35** | 0.34** | 0.10 |
| | Mother's occupation | 0.49** | 0.69** | 0.39** | 0.57** | 0.35** | 0.62** | 0.31** | 0.29* |
| 30–40 age | Father's occupation | 0.45** | 0.44** | 0.57** | 0.92** | 0.23* | 0.94** | 0.23* | 0.36** |
| | Mother's occupation | 0.32** | 0.65** | 0.56** | 0.64** | 0.51** | 0.74** | 0.39** | 0.45** |

*Source* Author's calculations based on Data Sources mentioned in the text
*Note* * and ** indicates significance at 1 and 5 % levels respectively

## Classes Within Class?

Are the *excluded castes* homogenous in terms of education, occupation, and mobility or do we also have classes within classes? It is evident that there are some differences within the *Excluded Castes* as regards their intergenerational mobility. The OBCs seem to be closest to the *Advanced Castes* in terms of achievements and mobility while the STs appear to be quite far off, indicating compartmentalisation even within the *Excluded Classes*.

In addition, educational mobility is higher for the urban people while occupational mobility is higher for the rural people. This indicates a perpetuation of urban–rural divide in terms of educational attainment along with occupational diversification in rural areas. Thus the rural areas are showing signs of continuity in terms of education and change in terms of avenues of livelihood. On the other

**Table 8** Derived mobility indices of occupational status in India—2004

Partial correlation of child's occupation after controlling for poverty status

| Age group | Location | Sch Tribe | | Sch Caste | | OBC | | General | |
|---|---|---|---|---|---|---|---|---|---|
| | | Boys | Girls | Boys | Girls | Boys | Girls | Boys | Girls |
| *1-digit NOC* | | | | | | | | | |
| All ages | Rural | 4.0 | 3.8 | 3.7 | 3.4 | 5.6 | 3.6 | 5.6 | 5.8 |
| | Urban | 3.0 | 2.1 | 2.5 | 2.9 | 4.0 | 2.6 | 4.7 | 4.4 |
| 20–30 age | Rural | 3.4 | 3.4 | 3.5 | 2.9 | 4.7 | 3.1 | 5.7 | 6.5 |
| | Urban | 2.7 | 1.8 | 2.5 | 4.1 | 3.4 | 2.6 | 5.3 | 7.4 |
| 30-age | Rural | 5.7 | 2.9 | 4.6 | 2.6 | 6.3 | 3.5 | 7.5 | 4.0 |
| | Urban | 5.4 | 2.7 | 2.4 | 1.3 | 3.6 | 1.4 | 6.2 | 4.0 |
| *Broad occupational group* | | | | | | | | | |
| All ages | Rural | 3.9 | 4.1 | 4.0 | 3.0 | 4.5 | 3.1 | 4.8 | 5.3 |
| | Urban | 2.9 | 1.9 | 2.1 | 1.9 | 2.9 | 2.0 | 4.9 | 3.7 |
| 20-age | Rural | 3.9 | 2.9 | 3.7 | 2.6 | 3.9 | 2.8 | 4.7 | 4.6 |
| | Urban | 2.4 | 1.7 | 2.2 | 2.3 | 2.7 | 2.1 | 3.1 | 5.1 |
| 30-age | Rural | 4.0 | 3.1 | 4.4 | 3.2 | 6.4 | 4.0 | 8.2 | 4.7 |
| | Urban | 2.6 | 1.8 | 1.8 | 1.3 | 2.7 | 1.2 | 3.2 | 2.5 |

*Source* Author's calculations based on Data Sources mentioned in the text
*Note* Mobility Indices are derived as inverse of the Average of the partial correlation coefficients of child's occupation with Father's and Mother's

hand, livelihood patterns in the urban areas are showing signs of continuity while educational scenario is changing. This simultaneous presence of continuity and change in human capital formation and labour market questions the sustainability of manpower situation in India.

The foregoing discussion also indicates divergence between different castes, gender and location in terms of both education and occupation as the privileged sections are also enjoying higher mobility and thus would progress faster compared to the laggards who also have lower mobility rates. Such social divergence in two of the fundamental areas—Education and Occupation—is apprehended to create similar trends in living standards as well. To find out causes of such stickiness among the excluded groups and bring out pragmatic solutions is the challenge facing the country.

## Reference

Driver ED (1962) Caste and occupational structure in Central India. Soc Forces 41–1:26–31

# Regional Dimensions of Mobility

One of the main features of a large country like India is its diversity in geography, culture, social structure and dynamics. All these diversities are reflected in regional disparities in socioeconomic pattern, including intergenerational mobility. There are regions where the lagging classes have improved tremendously over generations while there are also regions where educational and occupational statuses have shown stubborn stickiness. It is important to identify the dynamic regions and the stagnant regions so as to formulate policies based on regional experiences to make them more effective. We therefore explore the regional dimensions of mobility in India in this section.

## Regional Pattern of Educational Mobility

We have already noted that the all India average figure shows that in 1993 nearly 49 % of 20–40 age group persons, the generation of 'Children' in our study, have higher educational levels compared to their parents, which in itself is a substantial achievement. But there is significant interstate variation in upward educational mobility ranging from 84 % in Goa and 78 % in Kerala to 34 % in Bihar and 36 % in Rajasthan (Table 1). A higher mobility has been noticed in 2004 compared to 1993 for almost all the states but regional disparities remain high nonetheless. Goa, Daman, Kerala, Andaman, Assam, Manipur, Lakshadweep, Tripura, Nagaland, Pondicherry and Chandigarh are the states with higher upward educational mobility both in 1993 and 2004, while Madhya Pradesh, Rajasthan, Bihar are the states that are lagging behind.

Whereas upward educational mobility has improved significantly in Arunachal Pradesh, Sikkim, Uttaranchal, Himachal Pradesh, Jharkhand, Chhattisgarh, Karnataka, Tripura, Orissa, Punjab, Madhya Pradesh, Andhra Pradesh, Tamil Nadu, and Mizoram between 1993 and 2004, it has marginally deteriorated in Chandigarh, Goa, Jammu and Kashmir, and Daman and Diu.

Now if we look at the educational mobility according to social groups, we find that the disparities are quite high and varied across states. Consistently decent

R. Majumder, *Intergenerational Mobility*, SpringerBriefs in Economics,
DOI: 10.1007/978-81-322-1130-3_5, © The Author(s) 2013

**Table 1** Regional patterns of upward educational mobility

| States | 1993 | | | | | 2004 | | | | |
|---|---|---|---|---|---|---|---|---|---|---|
| | ST | SC | OBC | GEN | All | ST | SC | OBC | GEN | All |
| Andhra Pradesh | 25.4 | 41.8 | – | 46.2 | 44.3 | 25.7 | 58.4 | 52.8 | 59.0 | 54.5 |
| Bihar | 26.9 | 24.5 | – | 37.1 | 34.3 | 68.1 | 34.9 | 42.9 | 43.2 | 41.5 |
| Gujarat | 40.1 | 60.2 | – | 56.2 | 54.2 | 59.1 | 54.6 | 58.6 | 62.6 | 59.8 |
| Haryana | 77.9 | 52.8 | – | 52.6 | 52.8 | 18.0 | 62.1 | 61.2 | 58.3 | 59.9 |
| Himachal Pradesh | 30.7 | 59.4 | – | 60.7 | 59.2 | 74.3 | 79.3 | 76.6 | 73.7 | 75.7 |
| Karnataka | 43.3 | 36.2 | – | 47.6 | 45.8 | 54.9 | 57.4 | 58.6 | 61.7 | 59.3 |
| Kerala | 89.1 | 74.7 | – | 77.8 | 77.7 | 80.0 | 83.7 | 81.2 | 81.4 | 81.5 |
| Madhya Pradesh | 23.2 | 35.9 | – | 44.7 | 38.9 | 40.3 | 45.4 | 56.4 | 46.1 | 49.5 |
| Maharashtra | 43.7 | 54.5 | – | 60.1 | 58.3 | 50.5 | 65.4 | 66.4 | 65.9 | 65.0 |
| Punjab | 73.2 | 40.8 | – | 57.0 | 53.3 | 55.9 | 62.4 | 68.8 | 65.8 | 65.4 |
| Rajasthan | 28.4 | 26.8 | – | 38.7 | 35.9 | 39.5 | 46.7 | 46.2 | 45.5 | 45.2 |
| Tamil Nadu | 49.2 | 53.1 | – | 60.6 | 59.1 | 82.5 | 67.9 | 70.2 | 57.6 | 69.3 |
| Uttar Pradesh | 43.7 | 31.7 | – | 43.6 | 41.4 | 57.4 | 43.4 | 45.4 | 49.5 | 46.2 |
| West Bengal | 34.7 | 48.3 | – | 49.0 | 48.2 | 50.3 | 53.2 | 57.2 | 54.7 | 54.4 |
| Delhi | – | – | – | – | 0.0 | 66.5 | 47.3 | 51.7 | 48.3 | 48.6 |
| Orissa | 27.2 | 39.9 | – | 55.8 | 48.1 | 42.6 | 58.6 | 65.8 | 63.7 | 60.6 |
| Chhattisgarh | – | – | – | – | – | 48.4 | 59.7 | 56.8 | 53.7 | 54.4 |
| Jharkhand | – | – | – | – | – | 51.0 | 47.3 | 49.7 | 50.9 | 49.9 |
| Uttaranchal | – | – | – | – | – | 65.1 | 65.0 | 54.6 | 59.2 | 59.7 |
| Arunachal Pradesh | 55.0 | 50.0 | – | 37.1 | 41.7 | 65.5 | 100.0 | 1.6 | 51.3 | 61.6 |
| Assam | 59.6 | 65.8 | – | 66.7 | 65.8 | 77.0 | 63.1 | 73.8 | 68.3 | 70.7 |
| Goa | 0.0 | 78.4 | – | 85.4 | 84.6 | 20.0 | 86.9 | 86.8 | 76.4 | 75.6 |
| Jammu and Kashmir | 26.8 | 54.5 | – | 60.1 | 58.6 | 66.2 | 63.5 | 45.8 | 51.9 | 52.1 |
| Manipur | 67.6 | 100.0 | – | 70.5 | 69.7 | 69.9 | 89.7 | 62.3 | 67.8 | 66.1 |
| Meghalaya | 63.0 | 58.1 | – | 36.5 | 59.2 | 65.1 | 79.3 | 77.8 | 55.0 | 64.9 |
| Mizoram | 61.3 | 50.0 | – | 16.4 | 58.7 | 68.9 | 60.7 | 87.1 | 0.0 | 68.8 |
| Nagaland | 61.4 | 0.0 | – | 50.4 | 60.4 | 67.8 | – | 57.9 | 72.5 | 67.8 |
| Sikkim | 10.4 | 100.0 | – | 59.1 | 59.1 | 79.8 | 74.6 | 78.6 | 76.3 | 78.8 |
| Tripura | 57.7 | 63.0 | – | 62.7 | 62.1 | 76.8 | 70.6 | 77.0 | 74.8 | 74.7 |
| Andaman and Nicobar | 78.9 | 77.2 | – | 74.4 | 75.7 | 0.0 | 0.0 | 0.0 | 0.0 | 75.6 |
| Chandigarh | – | 82.5 | – | 68.3 | 71.0 | – | 55.6 | 42.0 | 38.2 | 43.5 |
| Dadra and NH | 36.4 | 82.3 | – | 33.9 | 41.9 | 80.6 | 1.9 | 89.3 | 73.1 | 75.9 |
| Daman and Diu | 60.6 | – | – | 84.4 | 82.7 | 92.1 | 11.1 | 46.3 | – | 76.6 |
| Lakshadweep | 63.9 | 50.0 | – | 100.0 | 62.8 | 62.7 | – | – | – | 62.7 |
| Pondicherry | – | 71.4 | – | 65.9 | 66.3 | – | 78.2 | 72.8 | 42.1 | 71.4 |

*Source* Author's calculations based on data sources mentioned in the text

upward educational mobility has been observed among Schedule Tribes in states like Kerala, Manipur, Meghalaya, Nagaland, Daman and Lakshadweep in both the periods 1993 and 2004. In Tamil Nadu, Punjab and Assam the situation for ST has improved during this period.

The percentage figures of ST children who have higher educational level compared to their parents has fluctuated very strangely in Haryana (77 % in 1993 to 18 % in 2004) and large improvement has been noticed in states like Bihar, Jammu &

Kashmir, Sikkim, Dadra, Himachal Pradesh. The upward educational mobility figure for the STs remains meagre in states like Madhya Pradesh, Andhra Pradesh, Rajasthan, Chhattisgarh, Orissa, and Goa, most of which have a substantial ST population.

Upward educational mobility among Scheduled Castes is high in Manipur, Sikkim, Chandigarh, Goa, Kerala, Tripura, and Pondicherry where substantial percentages of SC children have better educational level than their parents, both in 1993 and 2004. The situation of SC children have improved in Arunachal Pradesh, Meghalaya, Mizoram, Jammu and Kashmir, Himachal Pradesh, Haryana, Maharashtra, Punjab, and Tamil Nadu, whereas in states like Bihar, Madhya Pradesh, Rajasthan, Uttar Pradesh, and Orissa their condition has worsened.

The upward educational mobility for the Other Backward Classes can be calculated only for 2004 onwards as earlier studies do not enumerate them separately. Figures show that upward educational mobility among OBCs is significantly higher in Dadra, Mizoram, Goa, Kerala, Sikkim, Meghalaya, Tripura, Assam, Pondicherry, Tamil Nadu, Himachal Pradesh, Punjab, and Maharashtra. On the contrary, upward mobility is very poor in states like Arunachal Pradesh, Andaman and Nicobar, Chhattisgarh, Bihar, and Uttar Pradesh.

The regional patterns of upward educational mobility can be visualised from Figs. 1 and 2. It is amply clear that regions with high educational mobility are more abundant for the advanced classes compared to lagging classes.

## Regional Pattern of Occupational Mobility

Compared to the educational mobility, occupational attainment is much more sticky across generations. As noted earlier, we have considered both One-digit detailed Occupational Classes and Broad Occupational Grades. The national average upward occupational mobility in terms of One-digit Occupational Classes was about 13 % in 1993, increasing marginally to 15 % in 2004, indicating that only about one in every seven persons have better occupational level compared to their parents. Goa, Andaman, Chandigarh, Daman, Kerala, and Pondicherry are states where in both the periods substantially large numbers of children have higher occupation level than their parents (Table 2).

In Himachal Pradesh, West Bengal, Jammu and Kashmir, Nagaland, Tripura, Punjab, Jharkhand, Tamil Nadu, Delhi, Manipur, Uttaranchal, Orissa, Uttar Pradesh, Haryana, and Maharashtra, we observe only moderate upward mobility. On the other hand, occupational mobility of children is very poor in states like Mizoram, Meghalaya, Madhya Pradesh, Sikkim, Arunachal Pradesh, Assam, Bihar, Rajasthan, Andhra Pradesh, and Karnataka.

Occupational mobility scenario among socially excluded classes is lower than the average. For the Scheduled Tribes, upward occupational mobility during 1993 were quite depressing in almost all the states except a few like Lakshadweep, Punjab, Karnataka, West Bengal, and Himachal Pradesh where it was above national average. In states like Sikkim, Madhya Pradesh, Tamil Nadu, Andhra

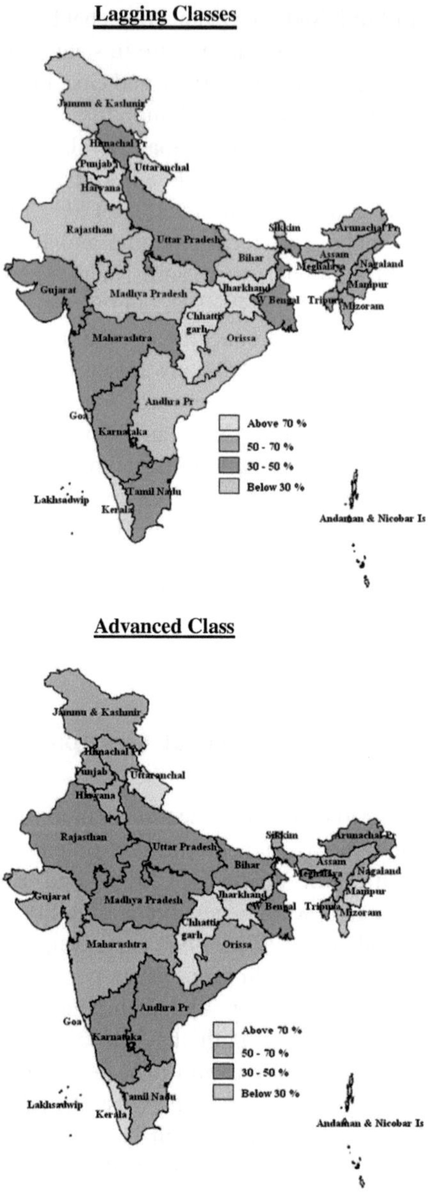


**Fig. 1** Upward educational mobility in Indian states—1993. *Source* Author's calculations, *Note* Map is indicative only

Pradesh, Bihar, Gujarat, Kerala, Orissa, and Mizoram occupational mobility remained less than 10 %, which is very low indeed. In the remaining states, mobility rates were between 10 and 13 %.

In 2004 however, only Kerala, Himachal Pradesh, and Gujarat exhibits mobility above 15 % while Andhra Pradesh, Chhattisgarh, Madhya Pradesh, Tamil Nadu,

Fig. 2 Upward educational mobility in Indian states—2004. *Source* Author's calculations, *Note* Map is indicative only

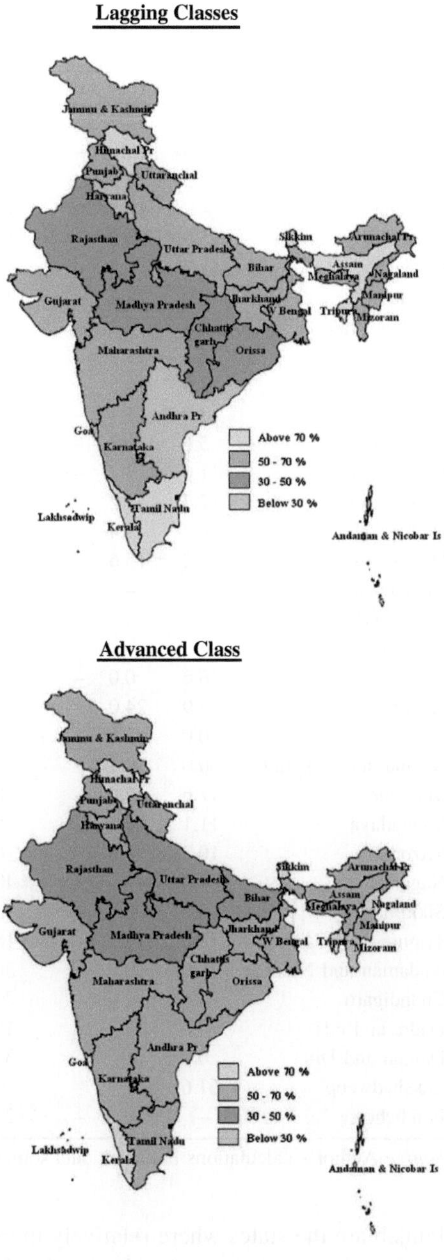


Maharashtra, Karnataka, Orissa, and West Bengal had mobility figures below 10 %. In other states occupational mobility varied among 10–15 % in 2004.

The occupational mobility rates of Scheduled Castes are again sluggish across most of the states in both the periods. Jammu and Kashmir, Kerala, Haryana,

**Table 2** Regional patterns of upward occupational mobility (1 digit NOC)

| States | 1993 | | | | | 2004 | | | | |
|---|---|---|---|---|---|---|---|---|---|---|
| | ST | SC | OBC | GEN | All | ST | SC | OBC | GEN | All |
| Andhra Pradesh | 7.6 | 14.7 | – | 11.6 | 11.6 | 6.7 | 12.7 | 13.5 | 14.3 | 13.2 |
| Bihar | 7.9 | 10.8 | – | 12.3 | 11.6 | 12.1 | 11.7 | 13.5 | 13.0 | 13.1 |
| Gujarat | 8.3 | 17.8 | – | 9.0 | 9.7 | 14.6 | 8.4 | 10.0 | 12.9 | 11.5 |
| Haryana | – | 16.5 | – | 12.4 | 13.0 | 13.1 | 21.0 | 19.0 | 10.6 | 15.2 |
| Himachal Pradesh | 15.9 | 25.2 | – | 12.5 | 15.1 | 29.3 | 19.3 | 26.3 | 21.7 | 22.0 |
| Karnataka | 18.7 | 5.7 | – | 12.2 | 11.6 | 7.5 | 19.8 | 12.1 | 15.5 | 14.3 |
| Kerala | 8.9 | 18.7 | – | 24.8 | 24.3 | 54.1 | 25.2 | 24.9 | 37.9 | 29.2 |
| Madhya Pradesh | 3.2 | 9.5 | – | 8.1 | 7.0 | 5.1 | 13.3 | 11.3 | 11.2 | 10.2 |
| Maharashtra | 5.5 | 21.7 | – | 14.5 | 14.1 | 9.2 | 16.6 | 12.6 | 17.4 | 15.0 |
| Punjab | 22.4 | 16.5 | – | 14.7 | 15.2 | 14.4 | 20.9 | 23.7 | 15.5 | 18.7 |
| Rajasthan | 7.0 | 11.1 | – | 11.2 | 10.5 | 11.0 | 10.1 | 11.4 | 23.8 | 13.2 |
| Tamil Nadu | 5.6 | 10.3 | – | 18.2 | 16.6 | 1.5 | 17.8 | 17.7 | 28.0 | 18.0 |
| Uttar Pradesh | 11.0 | 13.7 | – | 12.4 | 12.6 | 12.4 | 15.1 | 14.9 | 17.3 | 15.5 |
| West Bengal | 17.4 | 14.2 | – | 19.5 | 17.9 | 7.0 | 18.5 | 27.6 | 21.0 | 20.3 |
| Delhi | – | 4.4 | – | 19.3 | 18.1 | 0.0 | 6.7 | 39.9 | 18.1 | 17.1 |
| Orissa | 9.2 | 15.6 | – | 13.5 | 12.7 | 7.3 | 17.0 | 17.9 | 18.5 | 15.9 |
| Chhattisgarh | – | – | – | – | – | 6.5 | 16.4 | 12.1 | 12.1 | 10.8 |
| Jharkhand | – | – | – | – | – | 12.6 | 14.8 | 21.3 | 22.5 | 18.5 |
| Uttaranchal | – | – | – | – | – | 13.9 | 11.6 | 15.6 | 19.2 | 17.1 |
| Arunachal | 6.6 | 0.0 | – | 0.6 | 2.6 | 14.2 | 0.0 | 0.0 | 5.1 | 12.2 |
| Assam | 13.9 | 24.0 | – | 21.2 | 20.6 | 12.0 | 15.7 | 8.0 | 14.5 | 12.8 |
| Goa | 0.0 | 2.6 | – | 27.7 | 24.3 | – | – | 0.0 | 41.3 | 40.3 |
| Jammu and Kashmir | 0.0 | 30.7 | – | 20.0 | 22.2 | 16.7 | 21.6 | 19.2 | 20.3 | 20.2 |
| Manipur | 12.6 | 0.0 | – | 28.7 | 22.7 | 9.7 | 0.0 | 26.2 | 13.0 | 17.1 |
| Meghalaya | 11.1 | 26.5 | – | 5.0 | 10.6 | 11.3 | 0.0 | 0.4 | 29.0 | 11.6 |
| Mizoram | 10.3 | 0.0 | – | 0.0 | 9.6 | 8.7 | 25.8 | 0.0 | 0.0 | 8.7 |
| Nagaland | 18.0 | – | – | 48.0 | 18.8 | 19.0 | – | 16.8 | 25.3 | 19.1 |
| Sikkim | 0.0 | 100.0 | – | 13.5 | 15.1 | 8.4 | 17.9 | 13.7 | 0.0 | 10.7 |
| Tripura | 13.6 | 13.3 | – | 18.2 | 16.6 | 13.4 | 21.2 | 25.0 | 14.4 | 18.7 |
| Andaman and Nicobar | 28.0 | 50.0 | – | 36.0 | 33.3 | 0.0 | 0.0 | 0.0 | 0.0 | 37.8 |
| Chandigarh | – | 1.0 | – | 29.1 | 22.4 | – | 79.9 | 13.7 | 28.0 | 37.1 |
| Dadra and NH | 4.0 | 13.3 | – | 18.1 | 4.7 | 28.4 | 48.1 | 0.0 | 16.1 | 27.1 |
| Daman and Diu | 0.0 | – | – | 31.9 | 29.0 | 0.0 | 33.3 | 3.6 | 47.7 | 30.2 |
| Lakshadweep | 61.6 | – | – | 0.0 | 60.7 | 14.6 | – | – | – | 14.6 |
| Pondicherry | – | 0.0 | – | 21.9 | 21.4 | – | 12.3 | 23.5 | 46.2 | 23.3 |

*Source* Author's calculations based on data sources mentioned in the text

Punjab are the states where relatively more children have higher occupation class compared to their parents whereas in Bihar, Madhya Pradesh, Rajasthan, and Gujarat upward occupational mobility is very poor.

When we look at the occupational mobility of children compared to their parents in terms of broad occupational grades (White–Pink–Blue) it is found that mobility is further lower and occupational grades are very sticky in most of the

**Table 3** Regional patterns of upward occupational mobility (occupational grades)

| States | 1993 | | | | | 2004 | | | | |
|---|---|---|---|---|---|---|---|---|---|---|
| | ST | SC | OBC | GEN | All | ST | SC | OBC | GEN | All |
| Andhra Pradesh | 5.5 | 7.4 | – | 8.1 | 7.8 | 5.7 | 6.7 | 11.5 | 11.0 | 10.2 |
| Bihar | 5.2 | 7.8 | – | 10.5 | 9.5 | 12.1 | 9.3 | 10.9 | 12.6 | 10.8 |
| Gujarat | 6.3 | 11.9 | – | 6.9 | 7.2 | 8.2 | 3.5 | 7.9 | 10.7 | 8.3 |
| Haryana | – | 5.5 | – | 11.2 | 10.4 | 13.1 | 13.3 | 11.0 | 9.2 | 10.6 |
| Himachal Pradesh | 4.7 | 10.4 | – | 7.8 | 8.2 | 15.5 | 5.3 | 19.0 | 12.4 | 11.6 |
| Karnataka | 17.0 | 4.2 | – | 9.3 | 9.0 | 7.1 | 13.5 | 9.0 | 11.1 | 10.4 |
| Kerala | 8.9 | 14.1 | – | 20.5 | 20.0 | 54.1 | 17.0 | 21.6 | 33.9 | 25.3 |
| Madhya Pradesh | 2.6 | 4.8 | – | 5.3 | 4.5 | 3.0 | 8.4 | 7.4 | 9.7 | 7.0 |
| Maharashtra | 4.1 | 12.4 | – | 10.5 | 10.0 | 6.8 | 10.1 | 9.4 | 12.6 | 10.7 |
| Punjab | 5.2 | 8.8 | – | 11.6 | 10.8 | 14.4 | 10.6 | 19.0 | 12.3 | 13.2 |
| Rajasthan | 4.9 | 3.9 | – | 6.7 | 6.1 | 8.8 | 5.6 | 9.0 | 19.4 | 10.1 |
| Tamil Nadu | 5.6 | 8.0 | – | 13.7 | 12.6 | 1.5 | 12.9 | 13.3 | 17.0 | 13.3 |
| Uttar Pradesh | 11.0 | 6.5 | – | 9.8 | 9.2 | 5.4 | 6.4 | 11.1 | 15.9 | 11.2 |
| West Bengal | 5.3 | 10.9 | – | 16.2 | 14.1 | 4.7 | 16.1 | 22.6 | 16.0 | 16.1 |
| Delhi | – | 4.4 | – | 15.2 | 14.3 | 0.0 | 3.1 | 18.0 | 6.4 | 6.5 |
| Orissa | 6.4 | 12.0 | – | 10.6 | 9.7 | 4.7 | 13.5 | 15.6 | 14.9 | 13.0 |
| Chhattisgarh | – | – | – | – | – | 3.7 | 9.0 | 9.8 | 10.8 | 7.8 |
| Jharkhand | – | – | – | – | – | 6.8 | 8.4 | 15.3 | 13.8 | 12.1 |
| Uttaranchal | – | – | – | – | – | 13.9 | 4.3 | 11.8 | 16.2 | 13.3 |
| Arunachal | 6.6 | 0.0 | – | 0.6 | 2.6 | 11.0 | 0.0 | 0.0 | 2.7 | 9.3 |
| Assam | 12.2 | 21.3 | – | 19.5 | 18.9 | 11.6 | 15.7 | 7.3 | 12.5 | 11.6 |
| Goa | 0.0 | 0.0 | – | 16.5 | 14.2 | – | – | 0.0 | 37.0 | 36.1 |
| Jammu and Kashmir | 0.0 | 21.4 | – | 16.3 | 17.3 | 16.7 | 12.0 | 14.1 | 17.9 | 16.6 |
| Manipur | 11.4 | 0.0 | – | 26.5 | 20.9 | 8.0 | 0.0 | 18.4 | 11.1 | 12.6 |
| Meghalaya | 7.8 | 26.5 | – | 3.3 | 7.4 | 7.7 | 0.0 | 0.4 | 5.0 | 7.3 |
| Mizoram | 7.3 | 0.0 | – | 0.0 | 6.7 | 7.1 | 25.8 | 0.0 | 0.0 | 7.1 |
| Nagaland | 15.7 | – | – | 0.0 | 15.3 | 14.7 | – | 0.0 | 21.7 | 14.5 |
| Sikkim | 0.0 | 44.7 | – | 10.8 | 11.3 | 7.6 | 17.9 | 12.4 | 0.0 | 9.8 |
| Tripura | 9.8 | 10.6 | – | 16.2 | 14.3 | 9.7 | 14.3 | 23.7 | 11.7 | 14.9 |
| Andaman and Nicobar | 25.7 | 50.0 | – | 27.2 | 27.3 | 0.0 | 0.0 | 0.0 | 0.0 | 18.5 |
| Chandigarh | – | 1.0 | – | 6.8 | 5.4 | – | 52.1 | 2.2 | 19.8 | 23.8 |
| Dadra and NH | 3.9 | 13.3 | – | 18.1 | 4.6 | 28.4 | 0.0 | 0.0 | 13.9 | 25.0 |
| Daman and Diu | 0.0 | – | – | 31.9 | 29.0 | 0.0 | 33.3 | 3.6 | 47.7 | 30.2 |
| Lakshadweep | 42.1 | – | – | 0.0 | 41.4 | 11.9 | – | – | – | 11.9 |
| Pondicherry | – | 0.0 | – | 13.0 | 12.7 | – | 12.3 | 20.6 | 46.2 | 20.9 |

*Source* Author's calculations based on data sources mentioned in the text

states (Table 3). While, at the national level only 11.4 % children have higher occupational grade than their parents in 2004, at the state level only Kerala, Jammu and Kashmir, West Bengal, Tamil Nadu, Punjab, and Orissa have mobility figures above national average. The poor performing states in this regard are Sikkim, Arunachal Pradesh, Gujarat, Chhattisgarh, Meghalaya, Mizoram, Madhya Pradesh, Delhi, and Karnataka where upward mobility is less than 10 %.

Among the Scheduled Tribes, upward mobility at broad occupational grades is consistently poor in all the states both during 1993 and 2004. During 1993, mobility figures were lower than 10 % everywhere except in few states like Andaman and Nicobar, Karnataka, Assam, Uttar Pradesh, and Lakshadweep. In 2004 too, upward occupational mobility in excess of 10 % are observed only in Kerala, Himachal Pradesh, Nagaland, Punjab, Uttaranchal, Haryana, Bihar, Lakshadweep, Assam, and Arunachal Pradesh. For the Scheduled Castes occupational mobility at broad grade level are relatively better than the STs. At the regional level, the figures are higher than national average in the states of Sikkim, Kerala, West Bengal, Assam, Tripura, Karnataka, Orissa, and Mizoram both for 1993 and 2004. For the OBCs better performing states are Tripura, West Bengal, Kerala, Himachal Pradesh, Punjab, Manipur, Delhi, Orissa, Jharkhand, and Jammu and Kashmir, whereas in states like Arunachal Pradesh, Assam, Madhya Pradesh, Delhi, Gujarat, Rajasthan, and Karnataka upward mobility is lower compared to national average. Figures 3 and 4 provide a visual depiction of occupational mobility in Indian states and clearly bring out the regional disparity as well as that between social classes.

## Regional Pattern of Disparity Among Social Groups

So far we have considered the regional pattern of upward mobility in general and that of the excluded social groups in particular across the 1993–2004 period. However, we are more bothered about the disparity between the Excluded Groups and the Included Groups in terms of upward educational and occupational mobility. It has already been noted that mobility is higher among advanced classes compared to the excluded classes in the national level. We now discuss the trends exhibited by the difference between Mobility Figures for Advanced Class and that of the Excluded Classes in a regional setting.

It is observed that the national pattern is not universal and the situation is not same across all the states. Upward mobility of the advanced class is much higher than STs in states like Goa, Sikkim, Lakshadweep, Jammu and Kashmir, Himachal Pradesh, Orissa, Daman, Madhya Pradesh, and Andhra Pradesh in 1993. Moderate difference has been observed for Maharashtra, Gujarat, West Bengal, Tamil Nadu, Rajasthan, Bihar, Assam, Tripura, Karnataka, and Manipur. However, the reverse trend is also witnessed in states like UP, Dadra, Andaman, Nagaland, Kerala, Punjab, Arunachal Pradesh, Haryana, Meghalaya and Mizoram where mobility of STs are higher than the advanced classes. The magnitude of the difference in mobility among the two groups have decreased over the 1993–2004 period in most of the states, most notably in Sikkim, Jammu and Kashmir, Tamil Nadu, Lakshadweep, Bihar, Himachal Pradesh, Goa, Mizoram, Delhi, Daman and Diu, Assam, Madhya Pradesh, Gujarat, and West Bengal. However, in few states like Haryana, Punjab, Meghalaya, Nagaland, Kerala, Andhra Pradesh, Chhattisgarh, Andaman and Nicobar, Arunachal Pradesh, Karnataka the disparity between

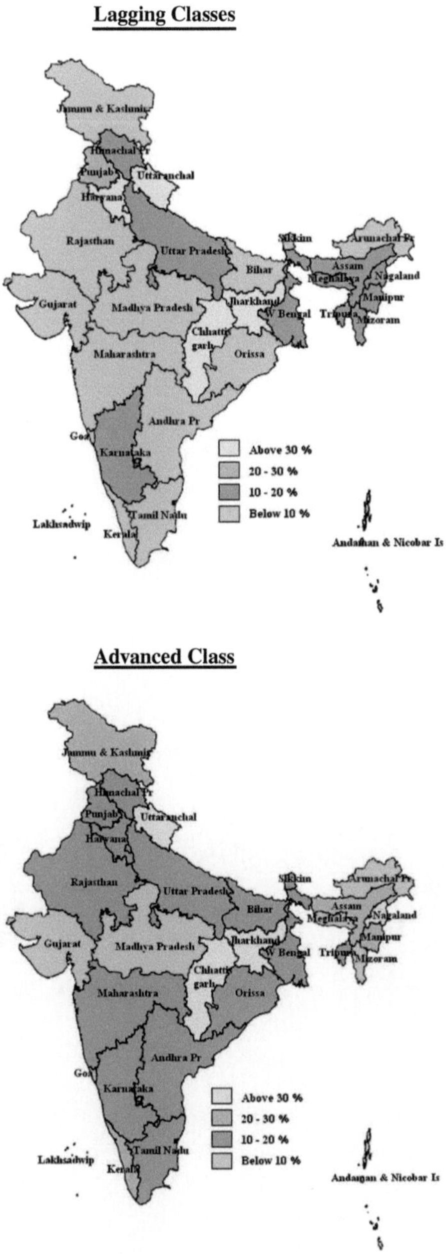


**Fig. 3** Upward occupational mobility in Indian states—1993. *Source* Author's calculations, *Note* Map is indicative only

mobility of advanced class and STs has either increased or turned positive from negative.

Similar trends have been witnessed for the Scheduled Castes though in almost all the cases the magnitude of disparity between the mobility of the advanced

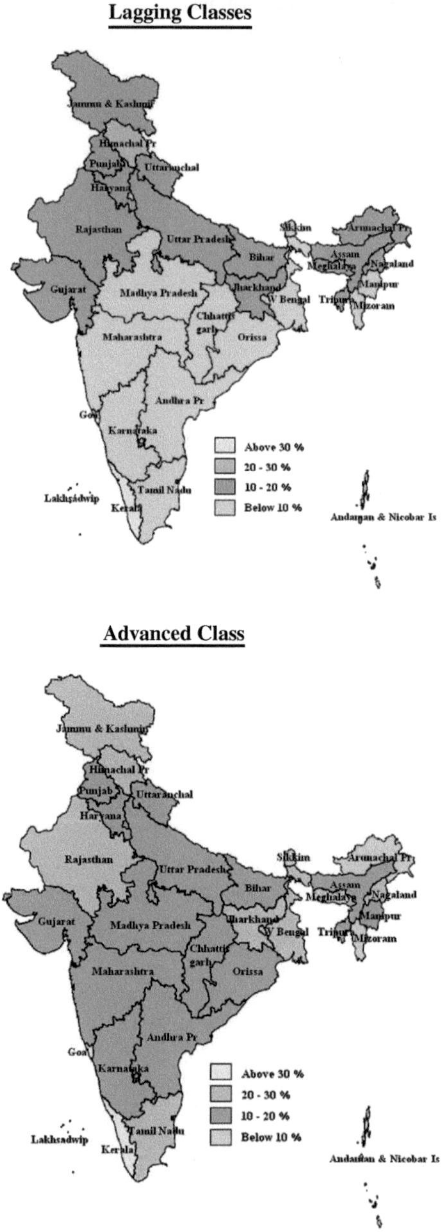


**Fig. 4** Upward occupational mobility in Indian states—2004. *Source* Author's calculations, *Note* Map is indicative only

classes and the SCs are less compared to that between the advanced class and the STs. The states where upward educational mobility of the SCs are substantially lower compared to the advanced classes are Nagaland, Punjab, Orissa, Bihar, Uttar Pradesh, Rajasthan, and Karnataka. The magnitudes of disparities have diminished in most of the states from 1993 to 2004, especially so in Nagaland, Lakshadweep, Arunachal Pradesh, Pondicherry, Mizoram, Tamil Nadu, Goa, Jammu and Kashmir, Chhattisgarh, Rajasthan, Punjab, and Orissa. On the contrary, the disparity has increased in Dadra, Daman and Diu, Sikkim, Gujarat, Manipur, Tripura, Assam, Jharkhand, Andaman and Nicobar, Delhi, and West Bengal.

For the OBCs the magnitude of disparity relative to the advanced classes is generally very low compared to that for the SCs and STs in most of the states. In fact, in most of the states upward mobility among OBCs is higher compared to the advanced classes. However, moderate disparity does exist in Daman, Arunachal Pradesh, Nagaland, Andhra Pradesh, Jammu and Kashmir, and Manipur; while marginal disparity exists in Kerala, Bihar, Jharkhand, Karnataka, Gujarat, Uttar Pradesh, and Uttaranchal.

Differences in upward occupational mobility between the advanced class and the STs are higher than national average in states like Delhi, Daman and Tamil Nadu in both 1993 and 2004. The reverse trend is also observed in Himachal Pradesh, Arunachal Pradesh, Kerala, and Mizoram, where occupational mobility of STs are higher than the advanced classes. Nagaland, Chandigarh, Jammu and Kashmir, Haryana, Manipur, Sikkim, and Kerala are states who have been able to reduce this gap substantially during 1993–2004. Unfortunately, in all the other major states the difference has increased in 2004 from the earlier level.

Similar features have been observed for the SCs as well. In states like Daman and Diu, Manipur, and Delhi occupational mobility of advanced classes are much higher than the SCs, which however have reduced over time. Moderate gap have been observed in West Bengal, Tripura Bihar, Uttar Pradesh, and Andhra Pradesh. In Dadra, Mizoram, Sikkim, Haryana, Tripura, Punjab, Karnataka, Chhattisgarh, Madhya Pradesh, Jammu and Kashmir, and Assam the SCs have higher mobility rates compared to the advanced classes. Over time however, gap between the mobility of the advanced classes and that of the SCs have increased in all the major states except Bihar, Madhya Pradesh, West Bengal, Delhi, Punjab, Chhattisgarh, Haryana, Karnataka.

The difference of mobility in occupational level between advanced classes and OBCs are higher only in Daman, Goa, Meghalaya, Pondicherry, Dadra, Chandigarh, Kerala, Rajasthan, and Tamil Nadu while in most of the other states OBCs have higher mobility than the advanced classes.

At the broad occupational grade level too, similar picture has been observed across the states. The difference in mobility between the advanced classes and the STs is much higher in states like Daman, West Bengal and Tamil Nadu. In contrast, mobility is higher for STs in Meghalaya, Arunachal Pradesh, and Mizoram. Sharp increase in such gap has been noticed in Lakshadweep, Nagaland, Daman, Karnataka, Uttar Pradesh, Rajasthan, Tamil Nadu, Chhattisgarh, Jharkhand, Delhi, and Orissa over the 1993 to 2004 period while in Kerala, Goa, Jammu and Kashmir, and Punjab the disparity has decreased significantly.

The difference in mobility between the advanced classes and the SCs is much higher than national average in Manipur and Pondicherry in both the periods whereas this gap has increased sharply in Kerala, Uttar Pradesh, Rajasthan,

Gujarat, and Maharashtra during 1993–2004. The gap has also reduced to a great extent in Chandigarh, Mizoram, and Haryana during the same period, resulting in reversing the earlier trend, i.e., mobility of SCs are now higher than the advanced classes in these states. Sikkim and Assam are the states where such reverse trend is observed in both the periods.

For the OBCs, grade level occupational mobility is higher than that of the advanced classes in most of the states except Sikkim, Tripura, Delhi, Manipur, West Bengal, Himachal Pradesh, Punjab, Haryana, Jharkhand, Orissa, and Andhra Pradesh.

## Regional Mobility: Causal Factors

What may be the factors that cause regional differences in mobility? Two factors come readily to mind—regional development level as indicated by regional per capita income (production), and state patronage to educational expansion as indicated by per capita government expenditure on education and training. While the former is a market oriented index, the latter is a measure of governmental intervention. To include a dynamic factor, we have also included growth in regional per capita income over the previous decade as a causal factor while exploring the mobility data.

It is observed that for the 1993–1994 period, educational mobility of the advanced class had significant positive association with regional income level and regional income growth over the previous decade (Table 4). It was also positively affected by state expenditure on education per capita. Educational mobility of the STs was positively associated with regional income growth. For the rest the associations are not significant, though positive. Occupational mobility during this period did not exhibit significant association with any of the causal factors that we examined.

During 2004 the situation was noticeable different. Educational mobility of all the social groups had strong positive association with state expenditure on education per capita, indicating that government efforts in expanding educational opportunities is a crucial ingredient of improving educational status across generations. Educational mobility of the advanced class was also significantly positively related to regional income level. What is noteworthy is that occupational mobility of the advanced class and the OBCs during this period exhibits strong positive association with regional income level. It thus appears that in recent times regional pattern of occupational mobility depends on the economic performance of the state or its developmental stage, though the benefit of expanding opportunities thrown up by market forces have been grabbed mostly by the top two classes of social hierarchy with the lagging classes being left out of this linkage.

The results underline the importance of government schemes and government financial support in pulling up educational standards across generations and the role of economic factors in determining occupational mobility, at least for some sections of the society.

**Table 4** Association of regional mobility with causal factors

| | Variable | Educational mobility | | | | | Occupational mobility | | | | |
|---|---|---|---|---|---|---|---|---|---|---|---|
| | | ST | SC | OBC | GEN | All | ST | SC | OBC | GEN | All |
| 1993 | PCNSDP | 0.24 | 0.04 | – | 0.52** | 0.19 | 0.06 | 0.14 | – | 0.26 | 0.14 |
| | | (0.29) | (0.88) | | (0.01) | (0.40) | (0.79) | (0.53) | | (0.24) | (0.53) |
| | Gr_PCNSDP | 0.39* | 0.21 | – | 0.35* | 0.07 | 0.06 | 0.04 | – | 0.07 | 0.04 |
| | | (0.09) | (0.38) | | (0.10) | (0.77) | (0.80) | (0.86) | | (0.78) | (0.87) |
| | PCEXPEDU | 0.08 | 0.20 | – | 0.65** | 0.23 | 0.25 | 0.07 | – | 0.12 | 0.22 |
| | | (0.79) | (0.47) | | (0.01) | (0.17) | (0.20) | (0.80) | | (0.67) | (0.44) |
| 2004 | PCNSDP | 0.11 | 0.18 | 0.07 | 0.65** | 0.29 | 0.24 | 0.01 | 0.38* | 0.32* | 0.34* |
| | | (0.63) | (0.43) | (0.76) | (0) | (0.18) | (0.29) | (0.97) | (0.08) | (0.10) | (0.10) |
| | Gr_PCNSDP | 0.17 | 0.23 | 0.16 | 0.09 | 0.13 | 0.26 | 0.08 | 0.13 | 0.16 | 0.13 |
| | | (0.46) | (0.31) | (0.49) | (0.69) | (0.58) | (0.25) | (0.74) | (0.56) | (0.49) | (0.57) |
| | PCEXPEDU | 0.47** | 0.64** | 0.64** | 0.67** | 0.64** | 0.16 | 0.03 | 0.08 | 0.29 | 0.01 |
| | | (0.04) | (0.01) | (0.01) | (0.01) | (0.01) | (0.51) | (0.9) | (0.73) | (0.21) | (0.98) |

*Source* Author's calculations based on data sources mentioned in the text
*Note* * and ** denotes significance at 5 and 10 % levels respectively; figures in parenthesis are significance levels

## Summary Observations

What transpires from the maze of regional trends is that there are vast regional disparities in intergenerational educational and occupational mobility in India. Such disparities are evident at aggregate levels of mobility, differential mobility rates for the excluded and advanced classes, and their time trends.

If we concentrate on the most recent available data, i.e., the 2004–2005 survey, we find that among the major states upward educational mobility and upward occupational mobility are both higher than national average in Kerala, Himachal Pradesh, Punjab, Karnataka, Orissa, Uttaranchal, and Tripura (Table 5). On the contrary, both these measures are lower than national average in the states of Bihar, Rajasthan, Madhya Pradesh, Uttar Pradesh, Chhattisgarh, and Andhra Pradesh. While Jharkhand, West Bengal, and Jammu and Kashmir have achieved higher occupational mobility but lower educational mobility, states like Sikkim, Assam, Maharashtra, Gujarat, Haryana, and Karnataka have higher educational mobility but lower occupational mobility. Recent unrest in some of the later group of states demanding more jobs for the locals may be direct fall out of such mismatch between enhanced educational achievements and lack of improved occupational opportunities.

In Tamil Nadu and Delhi disparity in terms of educational mobility is low but that in terms of occupational mobility is high (Table 6). On the other hand, in Haryana and Sikkim disparity is higher in terms of educational mobility but lower

**Table 5** Regional patterns of upward mobility—2004

| Educational mobility | Occupational mobility | |
|---|---|---|
| | High | Low |
| High | Kerala, Himachal Pradesh, Punjab, Karnataka, Orissa, Uttaranchal, Tripura | Sikkim, Assam, Maharashtra, Gujarat, Haryana, Karnataka |
| Low | Jharkhand, West Bengal, Jammu and Kashmir | Bihar, Rajasthan, Madhya Pradesh, Uttar Pradesh, Chhattisgarh, Andhra Pradesh |

*Source* Author's calculations based on data sources mentioned in the text

**Table 6** Disparity between upward mobility of advanced and excluded classes—2004

| Gap between educational mobility of advanced and excluded groups | Gap between occupational mobility of advanced and excluded groups | |
|---|---|---|
| | High | Low |
| High | Andhra Pradesh, Orissa, Maharashtra, Madhya Pradesh, West Bengal, Jharkhand | Haryana, Sikkim |
| Low | Tamil Nadu, Delhi | |

*Source* Author's calculations based on data sources mentioned in the text

in terms of occupational mobility. Surprisingly, in none of the major states the gap between advanced and excluded groups are low for both education and occupation, indicating that in almost all the regions the excluded groups are lagging in terms of either education or occupation, perhaps both.

A parallel can be drawn here between the social dynamics and economic dynamism of the regions. It is observed that in most of the economically stagnant regions, (Bihar, Rajasthan, Madhya Pradesh, Uttar Pradesh) social fluidity is also poor and both educational mobility and occupational mobility across generations are low. Social stagnation therefore goes hand in hand with economic sluggishness and spurt in the latter may be the key to inducing the former. This may also be the reason why the State in India has been attempting occupational transformation and livelihood promotion among the *excluded classes*, hoping to inject some vitality into the system.

# Intergenerational Mobility: Micro Level Study

We have so far analysed secondary data available at the macro level to bring out the situation of backward classes vis-à-vis the advanced classes in India in terms of Intergenerational Educational and Occupational Mobility. The results indicate that further probe is required to understand the process of mobility of the excluded groups. This is sought to be done through micro-level Field Studies. Focussing on five districts of South West Bengal, we first examine whether the pattern of intergenerational mobility evident at the macro level is also true in the study area. We shall then try to examine the role played by State support through various programs in enabling families to gain upward mobility.

## Survey Background

The field surveys were conducted in two parts over 2009–2010. First part of the Field Survey (Survey-I) was carried on in selected rural areas of five districts of West Bengal—Bardhaman, Birbhum, Bankura, Hooghly, and Purulia. While Bardhaman and Hooghly are developed districts, Birbhum and Bankura are moderately developed districts, and Purulia is a backward district declared by Planning Commission of India. Such a selection enables us to understand the role of regional economic conditions in affecting educational and occupational status of the people. This phase of the survey was an extensive one conducted through a set of Structured Questionnaire in the Households, mainly to estimate proportion of persons having different educational levels and in different occupations, separately for current and previous generations. The second part of the survey (Survey-II) was a more intensive one and was undertaken in parts of Bardhaman and Bankura districts to critically examine the situation of members of backward classes who have been provided financial support by the government for livelihood upliftment. In addition, various stakeholders like Government Officials, NGOs, members of SHGs and PRIs were interviewed to elicit information and opinion.

The descriptive structure of the Field Data is depicted in Table 1. In total, more than 19,000 persons from over 11,000 households were covered in the first phase.

R. Majumder, *Intergenerational Mobility*, SpringerBriefs in Economics,
DOI: 10.1007/978-81-322-1130-3_6, 

**Table 1** Descriptive features of field data

| Survey | Indicators | Bankura | Bardhaman | Birbhum | Hooghly | Purulia | Total SWB |
|---|---|---|---|---|---|---|---|
| First phase | Persons surveyed | 3,177 | 3,936 | 2,424 | 3,237 | 6,840 | 19,614 |
| Second phase | Persons surveyed | 189 | 245 | – | – | 172 | 606 |

*Source* Author's calculation based on field data collected during 2009–2010

The second phase was more of a case study in nature and about 125 households from three districts were surveyed to gather information about conditions of the backward classes, role of state support in occupational changes among these families, and how such support have changed their living including the educational status of the second generation. While most of the survey findings have been quantified, the essence of the second phase of survey is qualitative in nature and field experience and perception of the principal investigator plays a major role in arriving at the inferences and suggestions. The broad findings and their implications are discussed hereafter.

## Education Levels in Study Area

Levels of education in our study region (we call that rural SWB from here on) is worse than the state average, Literacy rate being about 65 % in 2009–2010. While Male literacy is about 71 %, Female Literacy is just below 60 % (Tables 2, 3, and 4).

At the spatial level, the situation is decidedly worse in Purulia, the district which is predominantly tribal, and relatively better in Hooghly and Bankura.

What is more striking is the difference in educational achievement levels between the backward classes (Hindu SC, Hindu ST, Hindu OBC, Muslim OBC and also Muslim General) and the advanced class (HUC—Hindu Upper caste). While literacy among HUC is more than 80 %, that among Muslim OBCs is less than 60 %. Similarly, proportion of High School passed is about 68 % among HUC and just about 10 % among the Muslims and SCs (Fig. 1a, b).

## Mobility Across Generations

The main focus of our study is the change in educational status across generations. It is observed that educational standards of the present generation are considerably better compared to the previous generation (Table 5). There are lesser number of Illiterates and more school pass outs among the present generation. However, the relative position of the backward classes is still behind that of the upper caste Hindus.

**Table 2** Educational status of the people in the districts according to social group (%)

| District | Education | Hindu upper | Hindu SC | Hindu ST | Hindu OBC | Muslim OBC | Muslim general | All persons |
|---|---|---|---|---|---|---|---|---|
| Bankura | Illiterate | 4.6 | 16.8 | 19.2 | 10.3 | 20.0 | 12.4 | 13.2 |
| | Lit below primary | 11.1 | 22.8 | 14.3 | 5.3 | 5.0 | 13.1 | 13.0 |
| | Primary passed | 37.8 | 31.3 | 27.3 | 22.8 | 25.0 | 26.3 | 29.7 |
| | Middle passed | 13.2 | 14.6 | 18.7 | 23.6 | 30.0 | 25.5 | 17.9 |
| | High school and above | 33.4 | 14.4 | 20.6 | 37.9 | 20.0 | 22.6 | 26.3 |
| Bardhaman | Illiterate | 13.7 | 52.5 | 39.6 | 25.7 | 24.7 | 40.8 | 31.7 |
| | Lit below primary | 8.5 | 13.7 | 11.0 | 13.9 | 5.4 | 30.5 | 16.8 |
| | Primary passed | 34.2 | 23.7 | 27.2 | 21.8 | 37.6 | 14.3 | 25.1 |
| | Middle passed | 6.6 | 4.1 | 11.7 | 11.9 | 12.9 | 7.8 | 7.7 |
| | High school and above | 36.9 | 6.0 | 10.5 | 26.7 | 19.4 | 6.6 | 18.6 |
| Birbhum | Illiterate | 2.4 | 21.4 | 11.5 | 42.3 | n.a. | 0.0 | 22.6 |
| | Lit below primary | 19.0 | 22.5 | 21.8 | 18.5 | n.a. | 25.0 | 20.6 |
| | Primary passed | 45.3 | 39.9 | 28.5 | 28.6 | n.a. | 75.0 | 35.4 |
| | Middle passed | 1.4 | 3.8 | 11.5 | 4.9 | n.a. | 0.0 | 5.1 |
| | High school and above | 32.0 | 12.3 | 26.7 | 5.6 | n.a. | 0.0 | 16.3 |
| Hooghly | Illiterate | 21.5 | 34.4 | 33.7 | 18.9 | 35.1 | 30.2 | 29.0 |
| | Lit below primary | 6.9 | 9.4 | 9.7 | 6.9 | 13.2 | 12.1 | 9.2 |
| | Primary passed | 24.4 | 24.8 | 26.4 | 23.9 | 27.6 | 35.0 | 26.5 |
| | Middle passed | 16.0 | 12.5 | 12.3 | 17.5 | 10.6 | 10.2 | 13.5 |
| | High school and above | 31.2 | 18.9 | 18.0 | 32.8 | 13.5 | 12.4 | 21.8 |
| Purulia | Illiterate | 30.6 | 52.8 | 54.2 | 54.6 | 57.6 | 41.6 | 52.6 |
| | Lit below primary | 10.6 | 12.4 | 12.1 | 9.8 | 13.9 | 16.9 | 11.6 |
| | Primary passed | 21.8 | 18.6 | 17.2 | 15.2 | 16.7 | 21.8 | 17.2 |
| | Middle passed | 14.3 | 8.5 | 8.6 | 8.1 | 5.9 | 10.7 | 8.6 |
| | High school and above | 22.7 | 7.7 | 7.9 | 12.3 | 5.8 | 9.1 | 10.0 |
| Study region | Illiterate | 17.5 | 41.1 | 37.2 | 37.6 | 43.1 | 34.5 | 34.9 |
| | Lit below primary | 8.7 | 14.2 | 10.9 | 9.1 | 13.0 | 18.1 | 11.4 |
| | Primary passed | 29.1 | 24.5 | 24.4 | 19.9 | 23.9 | 26.7 | 24.3 |
| | Middle passed | 12.7 | 8.9 | 11.8 | 12.3 | 9.1 | 10.1 | 11.4 |
| | High school and above | 32.0 | 11.3 | 15.8 | 21.1 | 10.9 | 10.5 | 18.0 |

*Source* Author's calculation based on field data collected during 2009–2010

**Table 3** Educational status of females in the districts according to social group (%)

| District | Education | Hindu upper | Hindu SC | Hindu ST | Hindu OBC | Muslim OBC | Muslim general | All persons |
|---|---|---|---|---|---|---|---|---|
| Bankura | Illiterate | 5.9 | 23.2 | 24.5 | 13.9 | 15.4 | 12.9 | 16.9 |
| | Lit below primary | 14.4 | 24.9 | 15.6 | 7.1 | 0.0 | 15.7 | 15.0 |
| | Primary passed | 37.3 | 29.5 | 25.6 | 26.5 | 15.4 | 24.3 | 29.2 |
| | Middle passed | 13.9 | 11.4 | 17.5 | 22.1 | 46.2 | 28.6 | 17.3 |
| | High school and above | 28.5 | 11.0 | 16.9 | 30.3 | 23.1 | 18.6 | 21.6 |
| Bardhaman | Illiterate | 11.9 | 58.3 | 49.1 | 32.0 | 28.3 | 44.4 | 34.8 |
| | Lit below primary | 11.5 | 16.2 | 9.3 | 14.0 | 2.2 | 28.1 | 17.1 |
| | Primary passed | 36.5 | 19.1 | 23.9 | 24.0 | 37.0 | 13.3 | 24.5 |
| | Middle passed | 6.3 | 3.8 | 11.1 | 8.0 | 15.2 | 8.5 | 7.7 |
| | High school and above | 33.7 | 2.6 | 6.6 | 22.0 | 17.4 | 5.6 | 15.9 |
| Birbhum | Illiterate | 3.7 | 28.1 | 15.2 | 52.8 | n.a. | 0.0 | 29.4 |
| | Lit below primary | 22.0 | 22.2 | 23.7 | 18.1 | n.a. | 0.0 | 21.1 |
| | Primary passed | 48.7 | 40.5 | 28.8 | 23.2 | n.a. | 100.0 | 34.5 |
| | Middle passed | 2.1 | 2.6 | 11.1 | 2.0 | n.a. | 0.0 | 3.8 |
| | High school and above | 23.6 | 6.7 | 21.2 | 4.0 | n.a. | 0.0 | 11.2 |
| Hooghly | Illiterate | 25.9 | 42.3 | 38.9 | 23.1 | 40.9 | 34.7 | 34.1 |
| | Lit below primary | 7.0 | 8.4 | 9.7 | 7.3 | 12.5 | 12.7 | 9.3 |
| | Primary passed | 24.6 | 21.1 | 24.9 | 25.6 | 25.4 | 31.6 | 25.5 |
| | Middle passed | 16.1 | 10.7 | 11.6 | 17.2 | 10.2 | 9.6 | 12.9 |
| | High school and above | 26.4 | 17.5 | 14.9 | 26.8 | 11.0 | 11.3 | 18.3 |
| Purulia | Illiterate | 41.7 | 64.8 | 64.7 | 61.9 | 65.0 | 55.3 | 62.3 |
| | Lit below primary | 12.1 | 12.0 | 12.0 | 10.8 | 15.5 | 18.9 | 12.1 |
| | Primary passed | 20.5 | 14.5 | 14.5 | 13.9 | 14.2 | 16.0 | 14.6 |
| | Middle passed | 10.6 | 5.0 | 5.9 | 6.7 | 2.3 | 6.9 | 6.1 |
| | High school and above | 15.2 | 3.5 | 2.9 | 6.6 | 2.8 | 2.9 | 4.9 |
| Study region | Illiterate | 20.7 | 50.7 | 43.7 | 43.5 | 49.0 | 40.0 | 41.0 |
| | Lit below primary | 10.1 | 14.0 | 10.9 | 9.8 | 13.0 | 18.2 | 11.8 |
| | Primary passed | 29.6 | 21.2 | 22.6 | 19.8 | 21.6 | 23.7 | 22.9 |
| | Middle passed | 12.6 | 6.3 | 10.6 | 11.3 | 7.9 | 9.5 | 10.3 |
| | High school and above | 27.1 | 7.6 | 12.1 | 15.6 | 8.4 | 8.6 | 14.0 |

*Source* Author's calculation based on field data collected during 2009–2010

**Table 4** Educational status of males in the districts according to social group (%)

| District | Education | Hindu upper | Hindu SC | Hindu ST | Hindu OBC | Muslim OBC | Muslim General | All persons |
|---|---|---|---|---|---|---|---|---|
| Bankura | Illiterate | 3.4 | 11.1 | 14.5 | 6.8 | 28.6 | 11.9 | 9.7 |
| | Lit below primary | 7.9 | 21.0 | 13.1 | 3.6 | 14.3 | 10.4 | 11.2 |
| | Primary passed | 38.2 | 32.8 | 28.7 | 19.2 | 42.9 | 28.4 | 30.1 |
| | Middle passed | 12.5 | 17.6 | 19.7 | 25.1 | 0.0 | 22.4 | 18.6 |
| | High school and above | 38.0 | 17.6 | 24.0 | 45.3 | 14.3 | 26.9 | 30.5 |
| Bardhaman | Illiterate | 15.4 | 47.0 | 29.6 | 19.6 | 21.3 | 37.2 | 28.7 |
| | Lit below primary | 5.7 | 11.3 | 12.8 | 13.7 | 8.5 | 32.9 | 16.5 |
| | Primary passed | 32.0 | 27.9 | 30.7 | 19.6 | 38.3 | 15.3 | 25.7 |
| | Middle passed | 6.9 | 4.5 | 12.4 | 15.7 | 10.6 | 7.1 | 7.7 |
| | High school and above | 40.0 | 9.3 | 14.6 | 31.4 | 21.3 | 7.6 | 21.4 |
| Birbhum | Illiterate | 1.3 | 15.7 | 8.4 | 32.4 | n.a | 0.0 | 16.6 |
| | Lit below primary | 16.5 | 22.8 | 20.3 | 19.0 | n.a | 33.3 | 20.1 |
| | Primary passed | 42.4 | 39.4 | 28.3 | 33.7 | n.a | 66.7 | 36.3 |
| | Middle passed | 0.9 | 4.9 | 11.8 | 7.8 | n.a | 0.0 | 6.3 |
| | High school and above | 39.0 | 17.2 | 31.2 | 7.2 | n.a | 0.0 | 20.7 |
| Hooghly | Illiterate | 17.2 | 27.1 | 28.5 | 14.8 | 29.2 | 25.9 | 24.1 |
| | Lit below primary | 6.8 | 10.3 | 9.6 | 6.6 | 13.8 | 11.5 | 9.1 |
| | Primary passed | 24.2 | 28.2 | 27.8 | 22.3 | 29.9 | 38.3 | 27.5 |
| | Middle passed | 15.9 | 14.2 | 13.0 | 17.8 | 11.1 | 10.8 | 14.0 |
| | High school and above | 35.9 | 20.3 | 21.1 | 38.6 | 16.0 | 13.5 | 25.3 |
| Purulia | Illiterate | 20.7 | 41.3 | 44.5 | 47.9 | 50.6 | 29.8 | 43.7 |
| | Lit below primary | 9.2 | 12.7 | 12.2 | 9.0 | 12.3 | 15.2 | 11.2 |
| | Primary passed | 23.1 | 22.6 | 19.7 | 16.3 | 19.0 | 26.7 | 19.5 |
| | Middle passed | 17.6 | 11.8 | 11.1 | 9.3 | 9.4 | 13.9 | 10.9 |
| | High school and above | 29.5 | 11.7 | 12.5 | 17.4 | 8.6 | 14.4 | 14.8 |
| Study region | Illiterate | 14.4 | 32.2 | 30.9 | 32.0 | 37.1 | 29.2 | 29.0 |
| | Lit below primary | 7.6 | 14.3 | 10.9 | 8.5 | 13.0 | 18.1 | 11.1 |
| | Primary passed | 28.6 | 27.6 | 26.0 | 19.9 | 26.1 | 29.7 | 25.6 |
| | Middle passed | 12.8 | 11.2 | 12.9 | 13.3 | 10.3 | 10.6 | 12.4 |
| | High school and above | 36.7 | 14.7 | 19.3 | 26.2 | 13.4 | 12.4 | 21.9 |

*Source* Author's calculation based on field data collected during 2009–2010

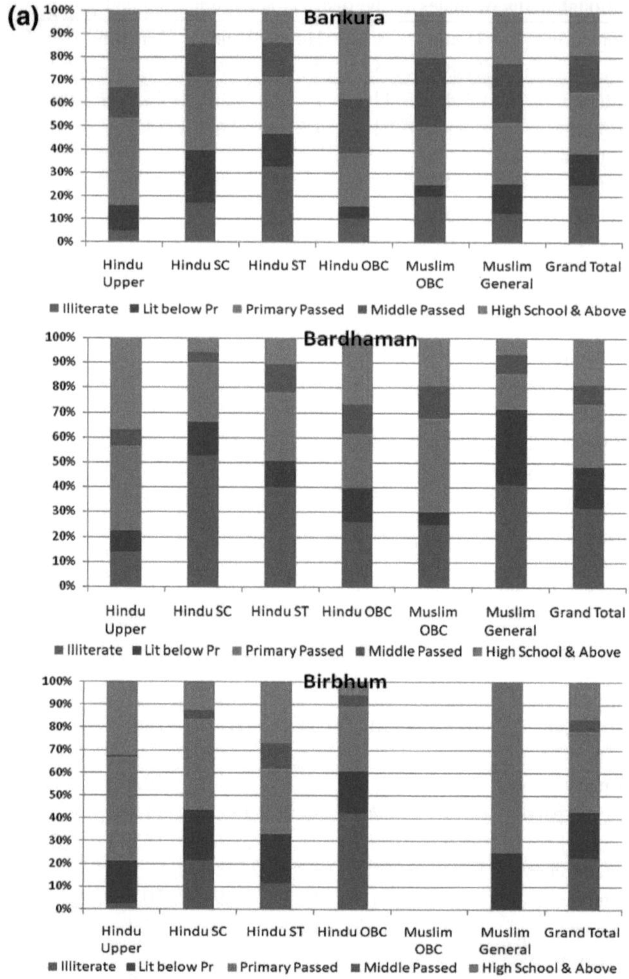


**Fig. 1 a, b** Educational status in the study region according to social groups (%). *Source* Author's calculation based on field data collected during 2009–2010

If we look at the Mobility matrix, it is evident that in sharp contrast to the national trends, upward educational mobility in the study region has been higher for the backward classes in all the districts except Birbhum (Table 6). Though such a result is mostly due to the initial low educational levels of the backward classes (in previous generation), it is heartening to note this result, indicating that the backward classes are breaking the traditional taboo and acquiring formal education quite substantially.

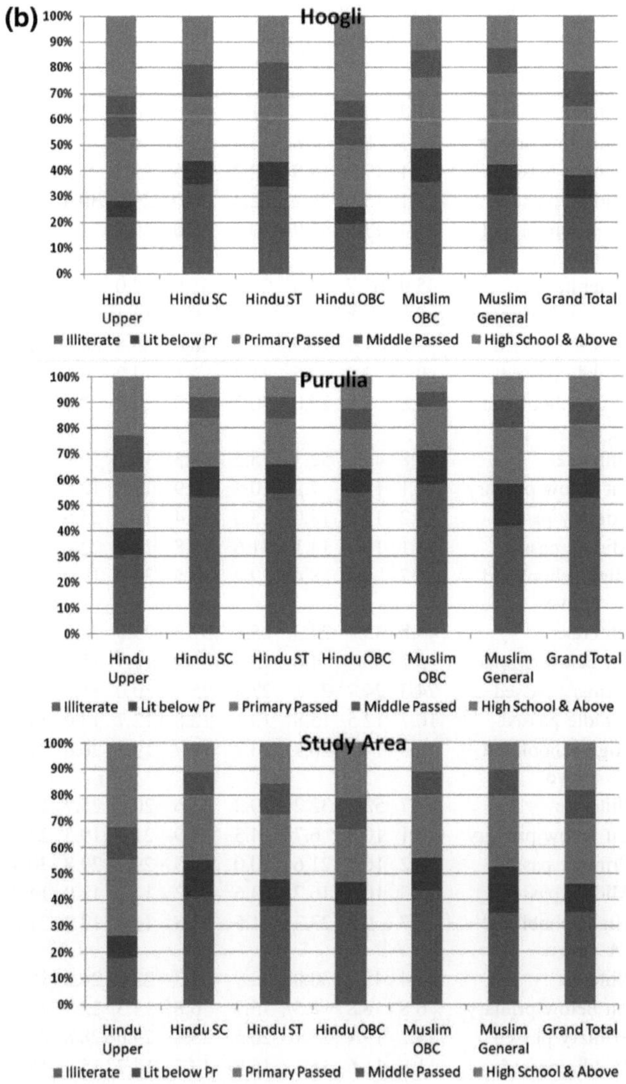


Fig. 1 continued

## Occupational Levels in Study Region

Distribution of occupation in our study region shows a predominance of the Grade-III occupations—Cultivation, Production, Transport, and others—among the rural population (Table 7). More than three-fourth of the 20+ population are engaged in such jobs, whereas the share of Grade-I occupations is only 13 %. The situation is relatively better in Hooghly where about one-fifth of the workers are in Grade-I jobs.

**Table 5** Educational status in the districts according to social group and generations (%)

| District | Education | Previous generation | | | | | Current generation | | | | |
|---|---|---|---|---|---|---|---|---|---|---|---|
| | | SC | ST | OBC | GEN | ALL | SC | ST | OBC | GEN | ALL |
| Bankura | Illiterate | 31.2 | 44.9 | 12.2 | 11.9 | 25.0 | 6.5 | 13.8 | 1.6 | 4.4 | 6.3 |
| | Lit below primary | 12.3 | 8.9 | 2.8 | 3.4 | 7.5 | 9.1 | 10.6 | 6.6 | 7.6 | 8.5 |
| | Primary passed | 16.1 | 17.8 | 18.8 | 22.2 | 18.5 | 25.1 | 21.5 | 21.3 | 18.1 | 21.9 |
| | Middle passed | 19.1 | 15.0 | 23.2 | 22.4 | 20.0 | 29.7 | 30.9 | 28.1 | 27.4 | 29.0 |
| | High school and above | 21.4 | 13.4 | 42.9 | 40.1 | 29.0 | 29.7 | 23.2 | 42.5 | 42.4 | 34.3 |
| Bardhaman | Illiterate | 45.9 | 63.7 | 34.5 | 20.3 | 33.9 | 19.0 | 39.3 | 16.5 | 10.2 | 15.6 |
| | Lit below primary | 5.8 | 6.8 | 4.3 | 7.0 | 9.3 | 13.1 | 18.6 | 9.6 | 13.5 | 24.2 |
| | Primary passed | 32.2 | 21.7 | 26.7 | 31.2 | 28.6 | 35.8 | 28.8 | 32.2 | 35.6 | 30.3 |
| | Middle passed | 9.3 | 2.0 | 9.5 | 11.3 | 9.1 | 17.2 | 6.1 | 15.7 | 8.6 | 9.6 |
| | High school and above | 6.8 | 5.8 | 25.0 | 30.2 | 19.0 | 14.9 | 7.1 | 26.1 | 32.1 | 20.3 |
| Birbhum | Illiterate | 27.8 | 44.1 | 52.3 | 15.2 | 38.5 | 18.1 | 19.2 | 29.3 | 10.3 | 20.4 |
| | Lit below primary | 13.1 | 13.1 | 7.2 | 10.4 | 10.9 | 13.7 | 12.8 | 19.6 | 9.1 | 14.3 |
| | Primary passed | 15.2 | 17.0 | 18.0 | 13.6 | 16.4 | 19.4 | 25.6 | 29.3 | 7.0 | 22.3 |
| | Middle passed | 18.1 | 16.4 | 14.1 | 31.6 | 18.8 | 16.3 | 22.4 | 11.9 | 33.9 | 20.3 |
| | High school and above | 25.7 | 9.4 | 8.4 | 29.2 | 15.5 | 32.6 | 19.9 | 9.9 | 39.7 | 22.6 |
| Hooghly | Illiterate | 44.8 | 45.1 | 27.3 | 25.4 | 37.3 | 25.0 | 22.8 | 18.9 | 20.0 | 22.6 |
| | Lit below primary | 5.2 | 3.3 | 4.8 | 5.3 | 5.0 | 12.9 | 12.2 | 11.1 | 10.1 | 11.9 |
| | Primary passed | 24.3 | 24.7 | 25.1 | 27.9 | 25.2 | 30.0 | 31.4 | 23.9 | 26.5 | 28.1 |
| | Middle passed | 10.7 | 12.5 | 15.8 | 15.2 | 12.8 | 12.7 | 13.0 | 14.8 | 14.2 | 13.5 |
| | High school and above | 15.0 | 14.5 | 26.9 | 26.2 | 19.7 | 19.3 | 20.6 | 31.3 | 29.2 | 23.9 |
| Purulia | Illiterate | 43.7 | 52.3 | 32.2 | 30.3 | 41.6 | 20.0 | 25.7 | 11.1 | 17.5 | 17.9 |
| | Lit below primary | 10.1 | 10.8 | 6.7 | 4.5 | 8.9 | 21.7 | 19.3 | 22.4 | 15.1 | 21.0 |
| | Primary passed | 20.2 | 16.4 | 21.6 | 20.0 | 19.5 | 29.4 | 29.8 | 30.4 | 24.0 | 29.6 |
| | Middle passed | 13.3 | 10.7 | 16.2 | 23.6 | 14.2 | 14.2 | 12.9 | 14.6 | 15.1 | 14.1 |
| | High school and above | 12.7 | 9.8 | 23.3 | 21.5 | 15.8 | 14.6 | 12.3 | 21.6 | 28.2 | 17.5 |
| Study region | Illiterate | 43.4 | 49.7 | 30.0 | 22.9 | 37.3 | 22.5 | 24.2 | 15.6 | 15.7 | 19.6 |
| | Lit below primary | 6.8 | 8.8 | 5.5 | 5.7 | 6.8 | 14.3 | 15.9 | 15.8 | 10.9 | 15.1 |
| | Primary passed | 23.2 | 19.1 | 23.1 | 26.5 | 23.1 | 29.6 | 28.8 | 26.8 | 26.2 | 27.9 |
| | Middle passed | 11.8 | 11.6 | 16.1 | 16.8 | 13.7 | 14.3 | 15.2 | 15.2 | 15.6 | 14.8 |
| | High school and above | 14.9 | 10.9 | 25.3 | 28.1 | 19.2 | 19.2 | 15.9 | 26.6 | 31.7 | 22.7 |

*Source* Author's calculation based on field data collected during 2009–2010

What is also significant, and noteworthy in terms of this research, is the disparity between the backward classes and the advanced classes in terms of occupational distribution. In all the districts, the proportion of workers in Grade-I jobs for upper caste Hindus is two to three times that of the SCs and STs. This disparity is the main factor behind lower livelihood and socioeconomic status of the backward classes in the SWB relative to the advanced classes since remuneration from the job is directly related to type of job in most cases.

**Table 6** Upward educational mobility in the districts according to social group (%)

| District | SC | ST | OBC | GEN | ALL |
|---|---|---|---|---|---|
| Bankura | 62.0 | 64.5 | 45.9 | 43.3 | 54.4 |
| Bardhaman | 59.0 | 45.6 | 51.4 | 45.6 | 47.7 |
| Birbhum | 49.8 | 59.3 | 45.8 | 50.4 | 52.1 |
| Hooghly | 52.6 | 52.6 | 50.7 | 49.6 | 51.6 |
| Purulia | 46.2 | 47.7 | 48.8 | 45.3 | 47.4 |
| Study region | 52.4 | 51.9 | 49.5 | 47.8 | 50.6 |

*Source* Author's calculation based on field data collected during 2009–2010

**Table 7** Occupational status of males in the districts according to social group (%)

| District | Activity group | SC | ST | OBC | GEN | All |
|---|---|---|---|---|---|---|
| Bankura | Grade-I | 7.8 | 5.6 | 24.8 | 20.4 | 14.5 |
| | Grade-II | 9.0 | 14.6 | 12.4 | 20.4 | 13.4 |
| | Grade-III | 83.3 | 79.8 | 62.8 | 59.2 | 72.2 |
| Bardhaman | Grade-I | 5.6 | 2.4 | 19.4 | 13.3 | 9.2 |
| | Grade-II | 5.6 | 1.9 | 6.0 | 5.0 | 4.5 |
| | Grade-III | 88.8 | 95.7 | 74.6 | 81.7 | 86.3 |
| Birbhum | Grade-I | 0.0 | 0.0 | 1.8 | 0.0 | 0.4 |
| | Grade-II | 0.0 | 0.0 | 0.0 | 0.0 | 0.0 |
| | Grade-III | 100.0 | 100.0 | 98.2 | 100.0 | 99.6 |
| Hooghly | Grade-I | 14.5 | 9.9 | 23.5 | 26.9 | 19.1 |
| | Grade-II | 12.7 | 9.2 | 22.0 | 18.3 | 15.8 |
| | Grade-III | 72.8 | 80.9 | 54.5 | 54.8 | 65.1 |
| Purulia | Grade-I | 3.2 | 1.3 | 4.3 | 9.3 | 3.9 |
| | Grade-II | 2.4 | 2.4 | 5.4 | 5.1 | 3.7 |
| | Grade-III | 94.4 | 96.3 | 90.3 | 85.6 | 92.4 |
| Study region | Grade-I | 10.8 | 4.2 | 14.4 | 21.3 | 13.1 |
| | Grade-II | 9.5 | 4.9 | 13.3 | 14.2 | 10.8 |
| | Grade-III | 79.7 | 91.0 | 72.3 | 64.5 | 76.1 |

*Source* Author's calculation based on field data collected during 2009–2010

## Occupational Mobility

If we look across generations, we find that there is only marginal improvement in the occupational distribution for the Present Generation relative to the Previous Generation (Table 8). In almost all cases there is a 2–5 % point increase in proportion of workers in Grade-I and Grade-II jobs and correspondingly a 3–5 % point drop in proportion of workers in Grade-III jobs, as we move from Previous to Present generation.

If we explore the occupational mobility situation, we observe that about 8 % of our surveyed population have better occupation than their parents (Table 9). Occupational mobility is highest in Hooghly and lowest in Birbhum. What is more striking though is the fact that in line with national trends, occupational mobility is

**Table 8** Occupational status in the districts according to social group and generations (%)

| District | Activity group | Previous generation | | | | | Present generation | | | | |
|---|---|---|---|---|---|---|---|---|---|---|---|
| | | SC | ST | OBC | GEN | All | SC | ST | OBC | GEN | All |
| Bankura | Grade-I | 7.8 | 5.1 | 22.8 | 28.6 | 15.0 | 9.8 | 5.4 | 21.4 | 19.4 | 12.7 |
| | Grade-II | 8.7 | 11.9 | 10.3 | 13.8 | 10.6 | 3.3 | 8.1 | 21.4 | 35.5 | 14.0 |
| | Grade-III | 83.4 | 83.0 | 66.9 | 57.6 | 74.3 | 86.9 | 86.5 | 57.1 | 45.2 | 73.2 |
| Bardha-man | Grade-I | 8.3 | 2.3 | 17.0 | 16.9 | 9.7 | 11.1 | 3.4 | 24.2 | 13.1 | 9.8 |
| | Grade-II | 3.7 | 0.4 | 4.3 | 3.4 | 3.6 | 5.8 | 1.7 | 12.1 | 5.4 | 5.6 |
| | Grade-III | 88.0 | 97.3 | 78.7 | 79.7 | 86.7 | 83.0 | 95.0 | 63.6 | 81.5 | 84.5 |
| Birbhum | Grade-I | 0.0 | 0.0 | 0.0 | 0.0 | 0.0 | 0.0 | 0.0 | 0.0 | 0.0 | 0.0 |
| | Grade-II | 0.0 | 0.0 | 0.0 | 0.0 | 0.0 | 0.0 | 0.0 | 0.0 | 0.0 | 0.0 |
| | Grade-III | 100.0 | 100.0 | 100.0 | 100.0 | 100.0 | 100.0 | 100.0 | 100.0 | 100.0 | 100.0 |
| Hooghly | Grade-I | 15.1 | 8.2 | 24.1 | 27.6 | 18.7 | 15.4 | 13.0 | 25.0 | 29.0 | 19.9 |
| | Grade-II | 9.5 | 6.8 | 16.4 | 17.2 | 12.1 | 13.0 | 8.4 | 19.5 | 20.1 | 15.4 |
| | Grade-III | 75.4 | 85.1 | 59.5 | 55.2 | 69.2 | 71.6 | 78.5 | 55.4 | 50.9 | 64.6 |
| Purulia | Grade-I | 3.0 | 1.8 | 4.2 | 15.2 | 3.9 | 3.7 | 1.0 | 5.9 | 21.2 | 4.7 |
| | Grade-II | 3.1 | 2.0 | 3.8 | 7.0 | 3.3 | 2.7 | 2.4 | 6.8 | 4.2 | 4.1 |
| | Grade-III | 93.9 | 96.2 | 92.0 | 77.8 | 92.8 | 93.6 | 96.6 | 87.3 | 74.6 | 91.3 |
| SWB | Grade-I | 11.4 | 3.6 | 13.3 | 24.4 | 12.6 | 11.8 | 4.5 | 15.4 | 25.1 | 13.5 |
| | Grade-II | 7.5 | 3.7 | 9.1 | 13.5 | 8.3 | 9.5 | 4.0 | 13.0 | 16.3 | 10.5 |
| | Grade-III | 81.1 | 92.7 | 77.6 | 62.1 | 79.2 | 78.7 | 91.5 | 71.6 | 58.6 | 76.0 |

*Source* Author's calculation based on field data collected during 2009–2010

**Table 9** Upward occupational mobility in the districts according to social group (%)

| District | SC | ST | OBC | GEN | ALL |
|---|---|---|---|---|---|
| Bankura | 0.0 | 4.5 | 20.0 | 25.0 | 6.8 |
| Bardhaman | 6.9 | 1.1 | 0.0 | 9.6 | 6.5 |
| Birbhum | 1.0 | 1.0 | 0.5 | 2.6 | 1.2 |
| Hooghly | 9.1 | 5.7 | 16.7 | 16.9 | 11.6 |
| Purulia | 4.3 | 1.9 | 6.3 | 11.5 | 4.6 |
| Study region | 7.3 | 2.7 | 10.7 | 14.7 | 8.3 |

*Source* Author's calculation based on field data collected during 2009–2010

substantially higher for upper caste Hindus compared to SC, ST, or OBCs. While mobility for the GEN group is close to 15 %, it is as low as about 3 % for the STs and about 7 % for the SCs.

## Observations

It thus transpires from our field survey that the condition of backward classes in the study region is considerably worse than the advanced classes in terms of not only educational standards or occupational distribution, but also in terms of mobility to higher stages across generations. However, educational mobility is higher among backward classes compared to the rest, indicating their lower initial levels as also the successful efforts of the local administration in bringing the children from families belonging to backward classes under the ambit of formal education. This educational mobility is not translated to occupational mobility though, and occupational stagnancy is a hallmark of the backward classes in the study region.

This is not surprising as discrimination along caste lines is very much true in rural India yet now. Asset holdings, especially land, are skewed in favour of the upward castes or advanced class. Villages are still segregated into neighbourhoods along caste lines. State allocation of resources and amenities are controlled by the members of the ruling class, who are predominantly from the upper castes. Hand pumps, wells, sanitation facilities, electricity are available in the upper caste neighbourhood, but less common in the *dalit* or tribal hamlet. Primary schools and health centres are situated within or near the upper caste *mohalla.* Members from the lower castes are often debarred from availing the facilities through physical segregation. While the barriers in attending government run schools have been overcome to a large extent, occupational segregation still remain. Job allocations are still along traditional family lines and efforts to come out of the shell are frowned upon. Institutional credit facilities remain elusive to members from lagging social classes as they are unable to arrange all the documents and collateral needed by officials. This dampens entrepreneurial activities among this section of the society and prevents occupational diversification. The state needs to look deeper into this aspect since the purpose of educational achievement shall be lost unless the formal training is converted to better occupation and livelihood status. Some of the steps taken by the government in this regard will be discussed in the next chapter to throw more light on the process of state support and how to make them more effective.

higher wages across generations. However, educational mobility is higher among [illegible]

[illegible]

# State Support and Occupational Change

## Role of State Support

It is evident from our field surveys, as well as the secondary macro data analysed earlier, that the occupational status of the backward classes are of substantially lower grade compared to that of the advanced classes. Moreover, members of the backward classes are observed to be stuck in parental occupation, most of which are blue collar Grade-III jobs, more frequently compared to others. Such occupational stagnancy and resultant poor livelihood quality is reflected in the inadequate educational status of the second generation family members. This educational backwardness traps them in low occupation as well, creating a vicious cycle of low occupation of parents–low education of children–low occupation of children.

To break such linkage, State must come forward to provide livelihood support to members of the backward classes so that they have a stable and sustainable livelihood, possibly better than their parents, and can afford to send their children to school. Various schemes are operational for supporting the members of SC and tribals communities in livelihood promotion. To understand the role played by the State, we decided to visit households that have benefitted from such schemes and examine whether state support have played any role in intergenerational mobility among them. In this section we briefly narrate our experience from the case studies.

## The Case Studies

Intensive field surveys were conducted in several locations spread across three districts in the second phase of our field studies. The experience from these case studies helped us in understanding the role played by state policies and support schemes in improving the occupational status of the people from the lagging social classes.

R. Majumder, *Intergenerational Mobility*, SpringerBriefs in Economics,
DOI: 10.1007/978-81-322-1130-3_7, 

## *Institutional Support for Occupational Promotion Among Backward Classes in Bardhaman District*

The first case study was in the far west corner of the district—in Rupnarayanpur GP of Salanpur CD Block of Asansol subdivision. Pratappur village was the first stop, a village with 125 households, of which more than 50 % are tribals. Two beneficiaries of AMSY scheme were selected for survey. These beneficiaries got financial assistance from WBSCSTDFC in 2004 for the purpose of starting a business of Goatery. They started with two goats initially and continued but they are not so successful in running the business. Annual addition to income is about ₹ 2,000 only and the beneficiaries now have one goat each. The goats were neither insured, nor were any infrastructural support made available. The support by the corporation seems to have had short-term impact. After that we spoke to other local people to have a brief idea of the economic condition of the villagers. The village was found to be very developed with availability of PHC, School, Pucca Road, Bank, Post Office, etc. But the villagers still lack basic amenities like safe drinking water and sanitation facilities. In fact, non-availability of water is related to unsafe sanitary practices also.

After Pratappur we went to Pithaikiyari village of Rupnarayanpur GP. This village has about 500 households, of which about 30 % are SCs and another 12 % are STs. This village is even more developed compared to Pratappur. Economic condition of the villagers is observed to be better. More than ten people from this village had received financial assistance under AMSY scheme in 2004. Most of them had started Piggery with the assistance. However, only two families are still in the business and we estimated about 10 pigs to be with those two families now. From the information obtained from those beneficiaries it was understood that the projects were not able to have any sustaining impact on the living condition of the Adivasis.

The second study was conducted in the south-west part of Burdwan District. Nandanpur village of Uchalan GP in Raina-II CD block of the district was chosen as this village had 17 beneficiaries of AMSY Scheme. The village had about 700 households, of which more than 35 % are SCs, and another 15 % are STs. The beneficiaries in this village got financial assistance in March, 2006 for the purpose of purchasing Cows. Our enquiry was whether this assistance has helped them to improve their livelihood. According to AMSY scheme they are supposed to get ₹ 10,000 of the total project cost as grant, which is non refundable, and the remaining amount as soft loan, refundable in next 6 years with an annual interest rate of just 3 %. However, it was learnt from the beneficiaries that they only received the cost incurred to purchase the cow as loan and the amount was to be refunded with interest. According to them, the grant was not released to them. Popular among agricultural families and cultivators, the business model was expected to yield a net benefit of ₹ 4,000 per annum to the beneficiaries over a three year cycle, after which they could get additional financial benefit from selling the calves borne to the cows.

We surveyed the 12 families who received financial assistance under AMSY scheme and 8 other families who require financial assistance but did not get it. Effectiveness of the AMSY scheme is mixed. None of the villagers considered this loan as a means to start or expand a sustainable business. While they claim that the complete business model was not explained to them, it was evident from their responses that they were also not interested in exploiting the venture commercially. They started this venture as this helped them to get additional milk for self-consumption, especially for their children. Probably the most important benefit from the scheme in this region is non-monetary since this has taken care of the nutritional level of their children. Some of the beneficiaries have partly refunded the loan while others have stopped payment after one/two instalments. It emerged that the lending bank had withheld the Grant portion of the loan apprehending that the beneficiaries will not repay the loan. While there may be some truth behind such apprehension, tinkering with a government scheme cannot be justified on such grounds as it is ethically wrong and undermines the economics of the whole project. It is good that this practice seems to have stopped since 2009. Members from the households who have not received any such assistance are of the opinion that loan or grant for purchasing Pickup Vans would be most helpful in enhancing their earning and ensuring livelihood security. But they are facing difficulties in securing such high value loans because of their dearth of assets and non-cooperation from bank managers and officials.

The village is well developed in terms of infrastructural availability like electricity, safe drinking water, road connectivity, etc. Recently the village was brought under the Rajiv Gandhi Rural Electrification Scheme and almost all the households are to get subsidised electric connection. Several of the surveyed households seem to be extremely poor, residing in run-down houses and are seeking financial assistance under Indira Awas Yojana. Regarding occupational pattern, most of the people work as agricultural labourers and also work under the MGNREGS. Significantly, successful implementation of MGNREGS was observed. Most of the surveyed people have got 100 days of work in the last year and they were of the opinion that the scheme should be modified to give them 200 days work in a year. Villagers used to face starvation during the months of December–March due to lean agricultural season, as demand for agricultural labourer was almost nil during this time. Hence they are suggesting that MGNREGS should be operative during this period so that they are assured of earning throughout the year. One more important thing that we have noted is despite having plenty of Rice Mills in the locality, these people are not getting absorbed in these industrial units. According to the villagers this is because of time constraints on part of the villagers, especially in the busy season, regular shift timings in the mill, and also because of lack of industrial skill among the villagers.

Regarding educational scenario, most of the children are found to be first generation learners and their parents are mostly illiterate or can just put their signature. Children were observed to be quite interested to study in formal schools, though they lack family support. Parents are also not confident about how long they will be able to finance their children's education, given the general poor livelihood status of the people. Educational infrastructure is satisfactory as the village has ICDS centre and both Primary and Secondary schools. Students are happy with the Mid Day Meal scheme and quality of the meal served to the students is also reported to be good. But health facility as well as the nutritional level of the children and adults is far from satisfactory. The villagers only have access to a Primary Health Centre at Uchalan which is 3 km away from the village, and villagers are demanding to set up a hospital at Uchalan as they have to rush either to Arambag or Burdwan for any major health disorder. Most of the child-births during last ten years were non-institutional, delivered at home, and without assistance of any trained personnel. As a result, child death during birth or within 15 days of birth was found frequent among surveyed families. Villagers do not have access to allopathic doctor on regular basis and they have to consult with RMP for minor illness. Nutritional level of the villagers are also poor and in 16 of the 20 surveyed households we found persons who are either currently suffering from Tuberculosis or have suffered from it in past. The problem of Anaemia was also found to be frequent, especially among pregnant women.

In all, the village needs focussed assistance in terms of health and sustainable livelihood skills.

The third case study was also in the eastern part of the district, conducted at Babla and Rampur of Uchalan GP. The village is located at the bank of River Darakeshwar, and is inhabited by Adivasis (STs). Occupationally these people are quite diversified—some are engaged as hired agricultural labourers, some as wage labourers at the nearby sand quarry in the river bed, some as fishermen, and some engaged in animal husbandry (piggery/goatery business). Better implementation of MGNREGS is also observed here as most of the people have got work for sufficient number of days in the current financial year. The village is well connected with two nearby trading centres—Uchalan and Eklakshmi. The villagers have been supported by various schemes of the Government like Adivasi Mahila Swashaktikaran Yojana (AMSY), Indira Awas Yojana (IAY), etc. The village being situated at the bank of river is very flood prone and quite a large number of houses get inundated and destroyed almost every year.

Educational infrastructure is sufficient, as there is a primary school in the village and a higher secondary school at a distance of about 3 km. In spite of this, Literacy status of the people is found to be very low and there are substantial numbers of *Out of School Children* who are found to be working to supplement their family income.

Nearest primary health care centre is located 4 km away at Paita. However, the health status of the villagers is not found to be satisfactory as most of the surveyed people are suffering from TB or malnutrition. Even though DOT is being provided free of cost by the Government, people are not quite aware of that and. Even those who are participating in the DOT, to be properly cured one have to take sufficient food supplementary, which they cannot afford. Other causes of poor health may be non-availability of proper sanitary system and safe drinking water in the village. Though electricity has already reached the village, most of the villagers could not afford to have electricity in their homes. Most of the financial supports received by the villagers under AMSY were used for purchasing cattle for self consumption of milk etc. Thus, here too, there was no significant impact of government support on livelihood and occupation of the beneficiaries.

Later in the day we went to Rampur, 7 km away from Uchalan GP to explore effectiveness of Self Help Groups in this region. An SHG in Rampur is engaged in producing Nutritional Supplements for children that are used by ICDS centres. The group is being run by 10 members since last 4 years and this nutritional supplement has become quite popular in the region with most of the ICDS centres in a range of 15–20 km using this product. The business plan, financial support, training and knowhow were provided by the local Panchayat in consultation with experts from ICDS and Government Health department. The members plan to expand their business and have applied to concerned authorities for allowing them to sell the product in open market under attractive packaging. Apart from this particular SHG we also visited several other SHGs who are engaged in the business of Grain Bank or Home-based Rice Milling (preparing rice from paddy) and selling that to the market. Almost all of them are running successful business with financial support from District Rural Development Cell. Some of these SHGs are run by SC/ST women and the governmental support has improved their livelihood status substantially. There is now almost no incidence of hunger and food insecurity in the village. Thus institutional support has changed the occupational pattern of the backward classes in this village up to a large extent.

The fourth case study was conducted at Kaiti and Chak Chandan villages of Kaiti GP in Bardhaman district. Pradhan of the Kaiti GP provided us with a brief overview of the villages under this GP, the activities of the Panchayat, and the steps taken by the socio-political groups of the area for improving the livelihood status of villagers in general and the tribals in particular. After getting an idea about the overall situation we decided to visit some of the villages and see for ourselves the ground reality. We started our field study with Gobindapur village. The village is agriculture based with cultivation being the major occupation of most of the people. With fertile land and good irrigation facility cultivators are capable of producing three crops in a year.

In terms of infrastructure the village doesn't have a pucca approach road and the villagers are yet to receive electric connection. The GP is trying to get electricity under RGRES for the tribal homes. The villagers are quite happy with the health infrastructure provided to them as the nearby RHC at Kaiti (3 km away) is fully functional with compassionate doctors and staff. The village has a Primary School and a *Madarsa* and the nearest high school is located at Kaiti. In this village we met the members of three successful Self Help Groups, Sathi Sayambhar Gosthi, Sundar Sayambhar Gosthi, and Jyoti Sayambhar Gosthi. All the thirty members are from ST families and are women, who had set up the SHGs independently in the year 2000. These SHGs started their economic activities with Grain Bank. After successful operation of grain banks for two years, they purchased a water body at a cost of ₹ 150,000 and started a fishery business. This venture was supported by the WBSCSTDFC and DRDC through grant and soft loan under several government schemes. There used to be a total production of

8–10 quintals of two types of fishes, Rohu and Katla. These fishes are sold in the retail market and they earn a profit of ₹ 20,000 a year. From their accumulated savings, they invested ₹ 100,000 in a fixed asset of a Submersible Water Pump and also make use of this water body for the business of supplying water to cultivators at the time of Boro cultivation. Water is being provided to approximately 60 Bighas of land for around 70 days in peak agricultural season at a price of ₹ 1,000/- per Bigha. By incurring a recurring expenditure of ₹ 30,000 per year the SHGs earn an annual profit of about ₹ 30,000 from this business. In addition, they have recently expanded to horticulture and planted Mango, *Jamun*, Jackfruit, and other trees alongside the water body. Interestingly, as a consequence of the formation of the SHGs, the financial condition of not only the members has improved, others have also benefited through trickledown effect. This was confirmed by examining the number of BPL families in this village currently compared to the first BPL Survey in 2003. Out of the 30 households of the members of the SHGs, 28 were below poverty line in 2003 while that number has decreased to just 3 presently. The villagers are of the opinion that inequality in income has also reduced to a great extent through this venture. While talking of the problems faced by the SHGs, villagers are of the opinion that they are really constrained by lack of electric supply as it would reduce their cost of running the submersible pump which would lead to higher profit margin. A lot of expansion plans like Poultry Business, House Dairy, Tissue Culture, etc. has been mentioned by the members. It was felt that if the SHGs are provided further loan/financial support to help them execute their expansion plans, they are in a position to substantially improve the occupational pattern and livelihood status of the villagers of this tribal dominated village.

The next stop was Chak-Chandan, nearly 4 km from Gobindapur. This village is mostly inhabited by people belonging to Minority Community (Muslims) and is well developed in terms of availability of safe drinking water (through Sajal Dhara Prakalpa), availability of electricity, availability of primary and high schools, etc. The villagers do access and can afford these infrastructural facilities, which has resulted in comfortable educational and health situation. Literacy is moderate, school drop-out is low, and immunisation is nearly full.

There we meet Meher Abjun Nesha, Resource Person of Kaiti GP. She, along with 10 associates is running an SHG since 2003 named Chakchandan Saban Sayambhar Gosthi. All members of this SHG are from the Muslim community. Initially they started with a Grain Bank (purchasing paddy when price is low, stocking that up, and selling when price becomes dearer, thereby earning profit; or using that as guarantee against food insecurity of the members during lean season). After having a successful Microfinance scheme for individual homestead economic activities, the SHG received their first Bank Loan of ₹ 20,000 in 2005 for Grain Bank. After repayment of first loan they received another loan of ₹ 50,000 in 2006 from UCO Bank at an annual rate of interest of 9.5 %. In 2010 they received a project of ₹ 141,000 under SGSY, out of which ₹ 1 lakh is subsidy and ₹ 41 thousand is soft loan. Each member took ₹ 10,000 for doing some business of their own and with the remaining ₹ 41,000 they had started a poultry. But due to sudden bird flu in the region they had to wind up the poultry. With the sell proceeds of the poultry they have purchased paddy of ₹ 60,000 and stocked up, and is expected to make a net profit of ₹ 90,000 from this grain bank. This is in addition to the member's own business profits. We visited some of the group members to examine their economic activity. Two members are engaged in Embroidery Work (*Jari*-work on *Sarees*) and have used their financial share of ₹ 10,000 to purchase looms etc. for their work. They work under subcontract at piece rate, materials and types of design being supplied by the manufacturer/trader. This is seasonal work with February–March, July–August–September, and December–January being the active period in the year. Two people can finish working on one *saree* in about 5 days and for that they are paid a sum of ₹ 700 on an average. Thus the two families earn about ₹ 14,000 each in a year from the economic activity started with State support. Some families are engaged in weaving bamboo mats and cotton quilts, selling those directly to the consumers. Input cost being very low and with own labour, the women of these families earn a handful of income from this business too. Thus state support has been able to improve the livelihood status of the beneficiaries in this village quite substantially and sustainable too. This is an excellent example how state support can enhance the educational and occupational status of backward section of the society if properly supported by the government through its various schemes.

## *Institutional Support for Occupational Promotion Among Backward Classes in Bankura District*

The first case study was Aamgarh, an interior village of Chhatna Block, habited mainly by ST families. Villagers don't have access to electricity, safe drinking water and none of the villagers has sanitary toilet in their house. There is an ICDS centre and a Primary School within the village.

Despite such infrastructural problem, especially lack of electricity and water, one significant thing that we observed among the villagers is consciousness towards education. Parents were observed to be conscious about their children's educational needs and they have taken the opportunities provided by schemes like KGBV, SSA, Student Stipend for backward classes, etc. though most of the people in the 40+ age group are illiterate, their children are educated. While most of the 20–40 age group persons have completed primary schooling, the children of the youngest generation are continuing to high schools.

In such a village we saw a Self Help Group named Rahir Adivasi Sayambhar Gosthi, who has started a Poultry with financial assistance from WBSCSTDFC. The infrastructure has already been setup and they are trying to make a contract with a private company for the purpose of supplying Chicks and marketing the grown up Broilers. All the members of the groups belong to ST community and are women. Each of the groups has obtained ₹ 1 lakh from the corporation as

**Table 1** Business model of poultry scheme

| Particulars | Years | | | | | | All total |
|---|---|---|---|---|---|---|---|
| | I | II | III | IV | V | VI | |
| *Costs* | | | | | | | |
| Capital expense | 130,000 | (borne by WBSCSTDFC as grant) | | | | | 130,000 |
| Recurring expense | | | | | | | |
| Chicks @ ₹ 13/- | 130,000 | 169,000 | 169,000 | 169,000 | 169,000 | 169,000 | 975,000 |
| Feed | 360,000 | 420,000 | 420,000 | 420,000 | 420,000 | 420,000 | 2,460,000 |
| Medicines/vet. charges | 20,000 | 25,000 | 25,000 | 25,000 | 25,000 | 25,000 | 145,000 |
| Water/electricity charges | 28,000 | 35,000 | 35,000 | 35,000 | 35,000 | 35,000 | 203,000 |
| Labour wages | 8,000 | 8,000 | 8,000 | 8,000 | 8,000 | 8,000 | 48,000 |
| Total recurring expenses | 546,000 | 657,000 | 657,000 | 657,000 | 657,000 | 657,000 | 3,831,000 |
| Total operating expenses | 546,000 | 657,000 | 657,000 | 657,000 | 657,000 | 657,000 | 3,831,000 |
| *Benefits* | | | | | | | |
| Sale of birds @ ₹ 60/- | 500,000 | 750,000 | 750,000 | 750,000 | 750,000 | 750,000 | 4,250,000 |
| Sale of manure | 9,000 | 13,000 | 13,000 | 13,000 | 13,000 | 7,000 | 68,000 |
| Sale of gunny bags | 5,000 | 6,000 | 6,000 | 6,000 | 6,000 | 6,000 | 35,000 |
| Total income | 514,000 | 769,000 | 769,000 | 769,000 | 769,000 | 763,000 | 4,353,000 |
| Net income | −32,000 | 112,000 | 112,000 | 112,000 | 112,000 | 106,000 | 522,000 |

*Source* Field Survey 2011

assistance and put up around ₹ 25 thousand from their own kitty. The poultries are started with around 1,200 chicks of which around 1,000 are expected to survive after 45 days. The business model (Table 1) is expected to yield a net profit of ₹ 22,500 each quarter, providing an annual income of ₹ 9,000 to each member of the group. The group members are very hopeful about their new business. There are 17 such groups in 5 villages around Chhatna who have started Poultries with assistance from WBSCSTDFC. We visited some other villages, and had similar experience.

Next, we went to the village Dha-danga near Subda More of Saltora Block, where WBSCSTDFC has assisted villagers in setting up Goateries. While electricity has reached the village, most of the people are so poor that they can't afford it. Sanitary toilets are present in most of the households, but are not regularly used due to shortage of water. Some villagers have taken a collective effort to construct a group and thereby to start a business so as to improve their financial condition. They have started the business of Goatery, purchased goats, insured them against illness and death, but the physical infrastructure is yet to be completed.

Each member had obtained ₹ 2,000 as assistance from the corporation and purchased 2 goats each. For the group, there are 18 does and 2 studs. They have also received ₹ 33,000 from the corporation to build up the physical infrastructure for the group (of 10 members) collectively.

The business model (Table 2) is expected to yield a net profit of ₹ 1.6 lakh over a 6-year cycle after leaving adequate capital for sustainable re-investment, providing an annual income of about ₹ 2,500 to each member.

**Table 2** Business model of goatery scheme

| Particulars | Years | | | | | | All total |
|---|---|---|---|---|---|---|---|
| | I | II | III | IV | V | VI | |
| *Costs* | | | | | | | |
| Capital expense | 55,000 | (borne by WBSCSTDFC as grant) | | | | | 55,000 |
| Recurring expenses | | | | | | | |
| Green fodder cultivation | 5,000 | 5,000 | 5,000 | 5,000 | 5,000 | 5,000 | 30,000 |
| Medicines/vet. charges | 1,000 | 1,000 | 1,000 | 1,000 | 1,000 | 1,000 | 6,000 |
| Insurance | 2,000 | 2,000 | 2,000 | 2,000 | 2,000 | 2,000 | 12,000 |
| Water/electricity charges | 1,000 | 1,000 | 1,000 | 1,000 | 1,000 | 1,000 | 6,000 |
| Labour wages | 8,000 | 8,000 | 8,000 | 8,000 | 8,000 | 8,000 | 48,000 |
| Total recurring expenses | 17,000 | 17,000 | 17,000 | 17,000 | 17,000 | 17,000 | 102,000 |
| Total operating expenses | 17,000 | 17,000 | 17,000 | 17,000 | 17,000 | 17,000 | 102,000 |
| *Benefits* | | | | | | | |
| Sale of animals | | | | | | | |
| Sale of adult Buck | 0 | 0 | 2,000 | 0 | 2,000 | 0 | 4,000 |
| Sale of adult Doe | 0 | 6,000 | 6,000 | 6,000 | 6,000 | 6,000 | 30,000 |
| Sale of buckling | 0 | 16,000 | 16,000 | 34,000 | 18,000 | 34,000 | 118,000 |
| Sale of doelings | 0 | 24,000 | 11,000 | 28,000 | 11,000 | 28,000 | 102,000 |
| Sale of gunny bags | 1,000 | 1,000 | 1,000 | 1,000 | 1,000 | 1,000 | 6,000 |
| Total income | 1,000 | 47,000 | 36,000 | 69,000 | 38,000 | 69,000 | 260,000 |
| Net income | −16,000 | 30,000 | 19,000 | 52,000 | 21,000 | 52,000 | 158,000 |

*Source* Field Survey 2011

The third case study was at Tetuliarakh village of Saltora Block. The village is situated in the foothills of Biharinath Hill. In this village WBSCSTDFC have provided financial support to villagers who have formed a SHG for producing traditional bamboo/cane baskets and allied products. Almost all the villagers are somehow associated with the SHG and are earning a steady though nominal income. They are basically making Baskets (*Jhuri, Kulo*) and different types of handicrafts from bamboo. But there is a problem of marketing as the nearest wholesale market is 15 km away at Burnpur, across the Damodar river. As a result the artisans have to carry their wares on head to the market. They have low bargaining power, and hence get low prices for their products though the retails prices are higher. If this problem can be corrected then artisans can make more money out of their business. In this village the educational scenario is not as good as we saw some dropped out children and some under age children were also observed to be engaged in making those handicrafts with their parents.

## Lessons from Field Studies

It thus transpires from several field studies that state support towards livelihood promotion of the backward classes have had mixed results in the study region. While in some areas and cases, there has been no sustainable long run impact on the occupational status; in some cases beneficiary households have been able to transform their occupation as well as livelihood status. This was most frequently also accompanied by attendance in educational institutions by the children of these families, an area that was unexplored by the elders of these groups. Thus state support towards livelihood promotion is indirectly leading to intergenerational mobility in education in the study region. What needs to be done to make these programs more successful is to draw up plans for sustainable livelihood shifts of the backward classes and not one time dole. Converging these schemes with other employment generation and capital creation schemes will also make them more effective. Another factor that acts as a positive ingredient regarding livelihood sustainability of the members from backward classes is that of traditional skill and family trade. People are comfortable with the skills that they have gathered from their parents and have practiced or seen to be practiced in their households. However, this factor also acts as a roadblock towards occupational mobility. Even projects and schemes from the WBSCSTDFC encourage people to take up occupations that require traditional family skills—e.g. Animal Husbandry, Handicrafts, etc. As a result, though the beneficiaries are provided funds for livelihood promotion, they remain stuck in their parental occupation. To come out of this cycle, state support should also be made available for skill promotion and skill diversification among backward classes. Entrepreneurship training, Vocational training, formation of skill development centres in the rural areas, and providing financial support for participating in such training programmes shall be helpful in breaking the low level occupational trap among the backward classes.

# Conclusion

## Summary of Findings

It is thus evident that upward mobility across generations in India is moderate for educational level and significantly low for occupational hierarchy. Though educational level of the second generation is higher than that of their parents, this is not adequately reflected in occupational mobility matrix. People are stuck in their parental occupational class and whatever movement is perceived is more often lateral—from one occupation to another within same broad occupational grade—than vertical. Mobility, by itself not substantial, is restricted mostly among the advanced classes and the historically excluded classes—Scheduled Castes, Scheduled Tribes, and Other Backward Classes—are exhibiting considerable stickiness in education and occupation over generations. Regional pattern suggests that mobility rates in general are lower in the lagging states. This lack of upward mobility in India, especially among the socially excluded classes and in the lagging regions, is a matter of grave concern. The fact that educational mobility is not being transformed to occupational mobility brings up the possibility of discrimination in the labour market. This also brings to fore the fact that historical discrimination and social exclusion have had a long run effect and it is very difficult to come out of this inertia.

State support in terms of financial grants for livelihood promotion among the backward classes seems to have a great role to play in this regard. In most of the cases where communities/households have obtained such support, the occupational stability has helped the present generation to achieve higher educational standards compared to their parents. Thus the vicious cycle of (low) parental occupation-parental education leading to low current education and occupation could be broken and intergenerational mobility was achieved. It is therefore expected that further expansion of such state support to the backward classes for their livelihood promotion and improving the condition of future generations will be pursued with greater thrust in coming days.

R. Majumder, *Intergenerational Mobility*, SpringerBriefs in Economics,
DOI: 10.1007/978-81-322-1130-3_8, © The Author(s) 2013

## Policy Recommendations

At the policy level, one must continue affirmative action in education by reserving certain number of seats for the backward classes so that their upward flow is not throttled prematurely. To ensure that all habitats are covered by formal schools where quality education is imparted would require opening of elementary schools in underserved areas. To encourage intergenerational mobility in education, opportunity cost of education, especially for the backward classes, a large proportion of whom also overlap the Below Poverty Line group, should be reduced. This needs subsidising elementary education, ensuring participatory classroom teaching, obviating the needs for private tuition for first generation learners, flexible school timings, and streamlining of the examination pattern. Occupational mobility is expected to follow educational mobility if labour market imperfections are not there. But discontinuity among these two, as evident from this study, indicates discrimination in the labour market which needs to be addressed. State support for livelihood promotion is expected to ensure occupational and educational mobility among backward classes. But field experience suggests that such schemes have resulted in income stability and educational mobility but reinforced occupational stagnancy because of their focus on traditional skill and family occupation of the beneficiaries. Out of the box thinking in designing such schemes and implementation is necessary to break this inertia. In this regard the Technical and Vocational Training Institutes and Entrepreneurship Development Programmes have a great role to play and the state should strengthen such extension programs. Such enabling actions must be supplemented by creating market incentives for occupational diversification. A recent decision by the government to encourage entrepreneurs from the excluded classes by earmarking a proportion of central government purchase from them is a bold and timely step in this regard.

It is hoped that the signs of dynamism evident among the excluded classes shall be boosted in times to come and *inclusive growth* will become a reality in India.

# About the Author

Dr. Rajarshi Majumder teaches economics at the University of Burdwan, West Bengal. Gold-medalist in both Graduation and Post-graduation, UGC Research Fellow, and a doctorate from the Centre for the Study of Regional Development, Jawaharlal Nehru University, he has written on issues related to infrastructure, regional development, labor, and social exclusion in both international and national journals. He also received the Sanjay Thakur Young Labour Economist Award from the Indian Society of Labour Economics for his research.


DOI: 10.1007/978-81-322-1130-3, 

MIX
Papier aus verantwortungsvollen Quellen
Paper from responsible sources
FSC® C105338

FSC
www.fsc.org

If you have any concerns about our products,
you can contact us on
**ProductSafety@springernature.com**

In case Publisher is established outside the EU,
the EU authorized representative is:
**Springer Nature Customer Service Center GmbH**
**Europaplatz 3, 69115 Heidelberg, Germany**

Printed by Libri Plureos GmbH
in Hamburg, Germany